Engaging Religious Education

LIVERPOOL HOPE UNIVERSITY STUDIES IN ETHICS SERIES
SERIES EDITOR: DR. DAVID TOREVELL
SERIES DEPUTY EDITOR: DR. JACQUI MILLER

VOLUME ONE:
ENGAGING RELIGIOUS EDUCATION
Editors: Joy Schmack, Matthew Thompson and David Torevell with Camilla Cole

VOLUME TWO:
RESERVOIRS OF HOPE: SUSTAINING SPIRITUALITY IN SCHOOL LEADERS
Author: Alan Flintham

VOLUME THREE:
LITERATURE AND ETHICS: FROM THE GREEN KNIGHT TO THE DARK KNIGHT
Editors: Steve Brie and William T. Rossiter

VOLUME FOUR:
POST-CONFLICT RECONSTRUCTION
Editor: Neil Ferguson

VOLUME FIVE:
FROM CRITIQUE TO ACTION:
THE PRACTICAL ETHICS OF THE ORGANIZATIONAL WORLD
Editors: David Weir and Nabil Sultan

VOLUME SIX:
A LIFE OF ETHICS AND PERFORMANCE
Editors: John Matthews and David Torevell

VOLUME SEVEN:
PROFESSIONAL ETHICS: EDUCATION FOR A HUMANE SOCIETY
Editors: Feng Su and Bart McGettrick

VOLUME EIGHT:
CATHOLIC EDUCATION: UNIVERSAL PRINCIPLES, LOCALLY APPLIED
Editor: Andrew B. Morris

Engaging Religious Education

Edited by

Joy Schmack, Matthew Thompson
and David Torevell with Camilla Cole

CAMBRIDGE
SCHOLARS
PUBLISHING

Engaging Religious Education,
Edited by Joy Schmack, Matthew Thompson and David Torevell with Camilla Cole

This book first published 2010. The present binding first published 2012.

Cambridge Scholars Publishing

12 Back Chapman Street, Newcastle upon Tyne, NE6 2XX, UK

British Library Cataloguing in Publication Data
A catalogue record for this book is available from the British Library

ISBN (10): 1-4438-3667-2, ISBN (13): 978-1-4438-3667-8

Contents

FOREWORD

Explicitly or implicitly, issues of ethics underpin every aspect of life, as public institutions and private individuals make decisions that will inform their own welfare and the lives of others. The ethical impulse and its determination has recently gained considerable intellectual attention, as many in the academy seek to understand the moral challenges and opportunities their own subject area presents. This series, which flows naturally from Liverpool Hope University's unique mission, is distinctive in its multidisciplinary range and encompasses arts and humanities, social sciences, business and education. Each volume is informed by the latest research and poses important questions for academics, students and all those who wish to reflect more deeply on the values inherent within different disciplines. Bringing together international subject specialists, the series explores the complexities of ethics, its theoretical analysis and its practical applications and through the breadth of contributing subjects, demonstrates that understanding ethics is central to contemporary scholarship.

Introduction

In the summer of 2009, Liverpool Hope University's PGCE Religious Education Department held a conference entitled *Engaging R.E.* A full range of stimulating workshops and a memorable opening keynote lecture by Professor Julian Stern were delivered, reflecting the breadth and depth of the University's mission to build on a unique heritage of over 160 years' experience in teacher training and an enduring commitment to teaching excellence. The ecumenical dimensions of that heritage, combined with its rooting in the realities of Liverpool life (with what many claim to be the UK's oldest multi-faith and multi-cultural community), ensure that the University is particularly well placed to help address the immense challenges and expectations placed upon education by a UK (and global) society appearing ever more insecure and uncertain about its values and direction.

It is noteworthy and fitting that religious education in particular has been placed in the forefront to deal with such uncertainties and encouraged to engage positively with fundamental educational and social issues that have strong ethical foundations. That is why the contributors to this volume are pleased to be involved in this timely and crucial debate. Clearly, any such involvement is a pressing one and not without difficulty and complexity. As religion returns to the centre stage of contemporary social and political struggles, the religious education teacher is thrust into the invidious role of expert facilitator and arbiter of an often tense encounter between divergent pressures from competing educational, political, and social goals (and the divergent ethical visions shaping their direction). These include the particularly sensitive and complex issues of social cohesion, equality, and diversity as well as pupil inclusion, all of which present the challenge of securing the lively and heartfelt response of pupils. Liverpool Hope University's *Engaging R.E.* conference revealed religious education practitioners rising to these challenges with characteristic commitment and insight.

As with the conference itself, the chapters presented here draw from as wide a range of perspectives as possible, including academic reflection upon competing pedagogical, philosophical and spiritual principles, as well as shared reflections upon the practicalities of classroom practice and curriculum content for those encountering these challenges on a daily basis. Teaching excellence is promoted when these perspectives meet and complement each other.

Julian Stern discusses pupil engagement with the fundamental realities of death and love. He elucidates a conceptual framework (drawing upon Buber and Macmurray's visions of the self understood in relationship with the other), to facilitate this process with a depth and sensitivity that allows for spiritually meaningful and edifying encounter with some of their most profound dimensions (including the Shoah). **Heather Marshall**, a classroom practitioner, considers the contemporary challenge of engaging R.E. pupils in combating islamophobia through exploring the concept of jihad in Islam. Following her exposition of some of the sensitivities and pressures (and subsequent confusion) that are brought to bear with respect to this topic, Heather produces very welcome practical strategies, including a scheme of work to support and guide colleagues in the classroom.

Robert Thorne, a sixth-form lecturer in religious studies, graciously shares the insights he gained with respect to engaging with community cohesion and Islamophobia at Oldham Sixth Form College in the wake of the disturbances in that city in the last decade. His honest analysis, rooted in this challenging context, provides inspirational, practical methodologies for promoting sincere, constructive dialogue between previously alienated and mutually suspicious communities and individuals. Enabling religious education effectively to engage with community cohesion also underlies **Joy Schmack**'s perceptive analysis of the effectiveness (or otherwise) of out of school visits to faith centres. Focussing on synagogue visits, the importance of planning objectives and the role of the "faith hosts" are clearly revealed. Key strategies are provided to help practitioners realize the huge potential value that the shared experience of a faith centre visit (and its faith representatives) can provide as a means for combatting negative stereotypes and promoting community cohesion.

Religious education is clearly now at the forefront of engaging with such issues as community cohesion and diversity. **James Holt** addresses the problem of how many faiths to cover within religious education. Given recent government emphasis upon understanding the full diversity of the local and national community, he cogently argues for the inclusion of New Religious Movements such as Latter-Day Saints and Jehovah's Witnesses (often numerically more prominent than Buddhists). In doing so, he raises important questions about the considerable pressures faced by religious education teachers to develop the expertise and resources required to present an increasingly wide variety of faith stances in a fair and objective manner. **Gaynor Pollard**'s chapter takes up the important challenge of feminism and religious education. She argues that those who produce agreed syllabuses in Religious Education often come from the more conservative wings of religious thought and practice and very rarely, if at all, take into account feminist theology. Her challenge is to situate what has been learnt from feminist approaches to religion into mainstream religious education content and teaching. Sharing examples from biblical teaching, she points to how pupils themselves might engage in a creative hermeneutics of sacred texts which takes their own gendered experience seriously. Drawing from the scholarship of Upton, she identifies three main approaches from within feminist apologetic responses to patriarchal norms, which encourage a reversal of more traditional methods of biblical work, so that the hidden voices of women might be reclaimed.

For many of the papers a central element of engaging pupils in religious education is the development of pupils' faculties of reflective analysis which, (with the recent re-emergence of child-centred educational philosophy) is once again understood in terms of the promotion of "pupil voice". An increasingly popular methodology being applied across many areas of religious education is the Philosophy for Children (P4C) strategy developed in the 1960s. Heather Marshall employs this to good effect with respect to studying jihad. **Pat Hannam** upholds P4C as the ideal approach for developing an inquiry-based, relevance-driven pedagogy for religious education that engages teenagers in meeting what she sees as the fundamental challenges of twenty-first-century society (globalization, diversity, and climate change). **Emma McVittie** also extols the virtues of reflective learning as a stimulus for creativity in both the training and classroom practice of primary RE teachers. She shares the successes of her application of individual reflective journals as a key motivational tool for developing creative teaching and engaging learning with her students.

Not surprisingly for religious education, the importance of the human heart emerged as a central theme in a number of the papers. **Matthew Thompson,** for example, draws attention to some of the secular philosophical frameworks and assumptions which he argues have come to dominate and distort the ways in which religions are presented and evaluated in the RE classroom. He describes what he holds to be a more authentic sacred philosophical framework (and a classroom resource) that allows for a more engaging encounter with the Christian faith. The vital challenge of engaging with depth as well as breadth of spiritual experience is reflected upon within a Catholic context by Daniel O'Leary and more generally by David

Torevell. **Daniel O'Leary** formulates his ideal vision of Christian education which focusses upon developing pupils' (and teachers') sacramental imagination. This concept (grounded in Newman's and Rahner's theology of nature and grace) is understood as an artistic awakening within the heart that facilitates sensitivity to, and a transforming encounter with, the Divine in our daily experience of the natural world. What in some respects can also be seen as this re-emergence of the more orthodox foundations of Catholic Christianity is also found in **David Torevell**'s exposition of a pedagogy of stillness, in which he draws upon the insights of the fourth-century Egyptian monk Evagrius. Both O'Leary and Torevell seek to counterbalance what they regard as the negative legacy of more traditional Augustinian (and potentially dualistic and demoralizing) Catholic understanding of sin and human nature. Torevell points towards a fascinating application of Evagrius' pedagogy of stillness as a means of promoting the kind of happiness and fulfilment which the Children's Society report of 2008 declares to be essential to children's well-being in the twenty-first century.

To be truly engaging, religious education must on the one hand facilitate an authentic, edifying encounter with as much depth and breadth of the richly diverse realities of religious traditions as time will permit. On the other hand, it also has to play its role in equipping pupils with the vision, skills, and motivation to engage effectively with the fullest range of challenges that they face in their personal and communal lives. Religious education practitioners are united in a love of their subject where these two dimensions of engagement so often complement each other. They bring their often divergent perspectives, yet also their shared commitment, to ensure their discipline remains the most critical component of any truly worthwhile and relevant education, thereby ensuring it plays a vital role in the moral and social development of pupils in the twenty-first century.

Camilla Cole, Joy Schmack, Matthew Thompson, David Torevell

Chapter One

Love, Death, and Inclusive Religious Education

Julian Stern

> Bravest thing about people, Miss Joan, is how they go on loving mortal beings after finding out there's such a thing as dying (Tyler, 1965: 76).

Professional practice in schools should be creating a healthy learning community in religious education, in which people are in genuine dialogue with each other and with people beyond the school. This paper describes how religious education (RE) is made more inclusive through its ability to deal with – to be in dialogue about – the deeply personal and challenging issues of love and death. Love and death are reasonably well established in RE syllabuses, as might be expected with such a subject that has so much potential to address these topics. For example, UK national guidance suggests that young children (aged 3 to 5) "talk about some of the ways that people show love and concern for others and why this is important" (QCA, 2004: 22). The same document suggests "discussing and reflecting on key questions of meaning and truth such as . . . life after death" (QCA, 2004: 14), and expects 7–11 year olds to address "the journey of life and death: why some occasions are sacred to believers, and what people think about life after death" (QCA, 2004: 27).

However, there are personal and professional reasons why love and death, and other sensitive issues, are often pushed to the sidelines, neutralized or distorted. These include limits set to dialogue, as the study of religions requires an "assumption of mutuality and dialogue"' (Hull, 1998: 190). As Jackson reminds us, RE is "a conversational process in which students, whatever their backgrounds, continuously interpret and reinterpret their own views in the light of what they study" (Jackson, 2004: 169).

Two philosophers illuminate the issues of love, death and dialogue: Martin Buber (1878–1965) and John Macmurray (1891–1976). Working from different religious perspectives (one Jewish, the other Christian), both of them are concerned with the personal relationships between people as the basis for understanding existence itself, and are therefore sometimes referred to as *personalist* philosophers (Long, 2000: chapter 11). For Buber and Macmurray, without love and without death there is neither life nor learning. The denial of love is the denial of the *other*; the denial of death is the denial of the *self*. This article builds on that broad insight to argue that good, engaging, inclusive, RE – what might be called *touching* RE – should be able to recognize both love and death. It is an attempt to understand and build a justification for RE out of the need to overcome the denial of love and death. Syllabus references are primarily to UK contexts, yet the underlying philosophy is much broader.

Denying Love, Denying Death

RE may be challenged if it is too *dangerous*; however, it is even more at risk if it is too *safe*. A group of UK primary teachers specializing in RE discussed David and Goliath. "I could not use that in my school", one teacher said. Asked why not, she said "because there is a killing in it, which goes unpunished". That was an interesting, but a safe, approach to RE. If schools were only to tackle the *safe* elements of religions, there would seem little point in studying religions. Neutralizing religious narratives can be found in school uses of Noah's ark: this account, the first biblical account of a holocaust, is often made into a jolly boating story with super furry animals. Explicit denial, in the case of David and Goliath, or neutralizing denial, in the case of Noah's ark, are liable to make the study of religions less significant – whether within religious traditions, or in multi-religious school-based RE. Both illustrate a disinclination to deal with death in RE, and there is a similar problem with love.

Love is difficult, and there are dangers in talking about love, bound up as it is with romantic and sentimental stereotypes. In recent years, the discipline of positive psychology has attempted to re-focus the larger discipline of psychology onto strengths and virtues, amongst which they count love. The description of love by Peterson (2006) is used as a starting point here, as it is detailed and authoritative (within its own discipline), and includes broader and narrower senses of love. Peterson's "typologies of love" starts with "affiliation", in which "the people involved simply want to be associated with some other person" (Peterson, 2006: 264), and goes through "liking", in which "the people involved have a positive attitude toward each other" (Peterson, 2006: 264), "friendship . . . [w]hen liking is coupled with a mutual perception of similarity and expectations of reciprocty and parity"'

(Peterson, 2006: 265), to the narrowly-defined love (Peterson, 2006: 267). Love, for Peterson, happens "[w]hen a relationship is characterized by reciprocated exclusiveness, absorption, predispositions to help one another, and interdependence" (Peterson, 2006: 267).

This description of love is in turn subdivided into "passionate" and "companionate" love (Peterson, 2006: 267), echoing the Ancient Greek and later Christian traditions of *eros* and *agape*, and Hindu traditions of kâma and *prema*. Hendrick and Hendrick, from the same disciplinary background, describe love in terms of self-expansion, and say that "[b]eing in love should result in higher self-esteem and stronger self-affirmation, as well as more other-affirmation", along with "'[p]ositive emotional states such as happiness and an optimistic outlook", "[h]ope for the future", and "a heightened sense of self-efficacy and the ability to cope with one's world" (Hendrick and Hendrick, in Snyder and Lopez, 2005: 481). Each element of these definitions could be argued over, yet the emphases on interdependence and self-expansion are helpful, at least as starting points.

Schools should not necessarily be places full of love (even in the broadest of Peterson's senses), any more than they should be full of death, but they should be places that allow for the *possibility* of love and friendship (Stern, 2009b: chapter 2), and that allow for the *consideration* of death and include forms of dialogue with dead people (Stern, 2009b: chapter 4). Where love and death are taboo or are actively denied, the school is not a real community. Existence in such places is *light*. Schools are not places where the slogan "Be yourself" is enough. To be yourself, you need others, and the self is not static: it grows and develops, moves outwards in self-expansion as love or friendship. "To be a friend is to be yourself for another person," says John Macmurray, and this "means stark reality between persons without pretence and sentimentality" rather than "the pretence to love" (Macmurray, 1979: 5).

The denial or neutralizing of death or of love, and the relationship of one to the other, is well articulated by the British poet Philip Larkin. Well known for his misanthropy as well as for his ability to express this sensitively and powerfully, Larkin's inability to love, or to love fully, seems to have been the source of much sadness. Larkin writes in the poem 'Dockery and Son' of the difference between himself and a friend from university (i.e. Dockery) who had a child at 19. Why have a child, why add to oneself? Larkin says, "Why did he think adding meant increase? / To me it was dilution" (Larkin, 1988; 153). He wrote another poem, when he was 33 years old, about himself as an individual, a one, and it is this that pins down his view of denial. "Thinking in terms of one / Is easily done" it starts, and goes on to describe a single life. "But counting up to two / Is harder to do; / For one must be denied / Before it's tried" (Larkin, 1988: 108). It is an interesting question to ask teachers of RE: are you able to count up to two, in the terms of Larkin's poem? Should teachers be attempting to help their pupils count up to two, too? One of Larkin's biographers says that Larkin believed "the adulthood of 'after twenty' has caused him to realize that solitude now involves effort; other people and the burden of being sociable have to be dealt with" (Bradford, 2005: 78). Counting up to two is not simply an alternative to the welcome, if increasingly difficult, solitude. It is also a description of love. Larkin wrote to a friend about his poem 'An Arundel Tomb'; "'love being stronger than death' is, he concludes, a 'sentiment . . . only justifiable if love can stop people dying', which, of course, it cannot" (Bradford, 2005: 153).

Love and death can be denied, or can be distorted. A writer on the Afghanistan conflict describes a kind of distorted view of love or, rather, two kinds of distorted views of love:

> In the first week of the war in Afghanistan, a British newspaper reporter spoke to a Taliban fighter on the Pakistani border. The young *jihadi* was full of confidence. The Americans, he said, would never win, for "they love Pepsi-Cola, but we love death." (Buruma and Margalit, 2004: 49)

Surely a love of Pepsi-Cola and a love of death are equally problematic, and each represents a denial of the more obvious characteristics of love. Another denial would be to enforce love, and this seems to be the message described in the following extract from the writings of Rudolf Steiner:

> It is December 21, 1919, and Rudolf Steiner is addressing a Christmas assembly of teachers, parents, and students of the newly formed Waldorf School. "Do you love your teachers?" he asks the children. "Yes," comes the resounding reply. A few minutes later in his talk he repeats, "... I would like to ask you again, 'Don't you all sincerely love your teachers?'" "Yes, we do," shout the children. These earnest questions and fervent answers are repeated many times in the next few years on his frequent visits to the school. (Steiner, 1996: ix)

Perhaps something is lost in the translation, but the sense of enforced love suggested by this report is uncomfortable and seems as much a denial of real love as that described by Larkin.

Overcoming Denial: Philosophers

Is it possible for RE to help overcome the denial of love and death? Such a task is clearly not easy, and is not exclusive to RE. However, the task is made easier through understanding the approach to persons provided by two philosophers, the Scottish Christian writer John Macmurray, and the Viennese-born Jewish writer Martin Buber. For Macmurray, a human being "knows that he is alive, and consequently knows that he must die", and this knowledge "is the first inevitable consequence of being a person" (Macmurray, 1935: 37). "The fear of death isolates man from the world," he continues, and "isolates man from man, breaking the bonds between friends and kinsmen, and forcing the individual into the isolation of his own existence" (Macmurray, 1935: 37), yet at the same time it "reveals the intimate dependence of man on nature and upon his fellows" so that, "[u]nless this consciousness of death were overcome, human life would be paralysed" (Macmurray, 1935: 37). It is religion, according to Macmurray, that captures the effort to "deal with the knowledge of death and to overcome the fear of it" (Macmurray, 1935: 37–8), but not through denial. In fact it was in the trenches of World War One that he learnt to overcome that fear.

> Just outside my post in the front line itself a dead Highlander, in a full kilted uniform, was hung up in the centre of a mass of barbed wire. It was impossible to get at him without a major operation in no man's land. So there he remained, day after day, almost as if he were one of us. No doubt this normal experience of the soldier on active service affects men differently. With me it resulted in a quick and complete acceptance of death, for myself as well as for my comrades. It had seemed a dreaded end, before the war. Now it became an incident in life, and in the result it removed for ever the *fear* of death. (Macmurray, 1995: 18)

It is worth noting that this is not overcoming the fear of death by denying it, or by denying its unpleasantness, but rather by recognising how the fear of death would restrict life: "[t]he person who lives on the defensive is really seeking death, seeking to escape from life", and this applies to "most of us", who "wake up late in life to discover that we have never really lived at all" (Macmurray, 1996: 144). The knowledge of death is also the knowledge of being embodied, as Hull says of spirituality: "[s]pirituality is not the antithesis of materialism . . . [so a] true spirituality will not seek to become more and more spiritual but will seek to become more and more embodied, more significantly in touch with our bodily existences" (Hull, 1998: 65). If the fear of death can restrict or neutralize life, the appropriate response to such fear is to wake up and to take part in life. This is done with other people – for Macmurray, other people in community, people we treat as ends in themselves and not as means to other ends. Communities are where people are and can become more real. "We are all more or less unreal", he says, and "[o]ur business is to make ourselves a little more real than we are" (Macmurray, 1992: 143). Schools are places in which this should happen, as schools – like families, friendship groups, and religious groups – are necessarily communities.

Macmurray says that "[t]he school is a community; and we learn to live in community only by living in a community" (Macmurray, 1968: 149–50). A school's "first principle is that it must be a real community" (Macmurray, 1968: 35). This is "[n]ot because community is a good thing – I would underline this – but because this is the condition of success in its educational function" (Macmurray, 1968: 35). Hence

> when we try to teach, we must deal with living human beings. We, the teachers, are persons. Those whom we would teach are persons. We must meet them face to face, in a personal intercourse. This is the primary fact about education. It is one of the forms of personal relationship. It is a continuing personal exchange between two generations. To assert this is by no means to define an ideal, but to state a fact. It declares not what education ought to be, but what it is – and is inescapably. We may ignore this fact; we may imagine that our task is of a different order; but this will make no difference to what is actually taking place. We may act as though we were teaching arithmetic or history. In fact we are teaching *people*. The arithmetic or the history is merely a medium through which a personal intercourse is established and maintained. (Macmurray, 1968: 5)

The difference between an organization in which people can become more real and one in which this is less likely to happen is well illustrated by Martin Buber. Buber considered the problem of treating people as *it*, matched by an equally problematic approach to an exclusively private life of feelings. Both positions need to be overcome. In modern society, he said, all too often:

> Institutions are "outside," where all sorts of aims are pursued, where a man works, negotiates, bears influence, undertakes, concurs, organises, conducts business, officiates, preaches. They are the tolerably well-ordered and to some extent harmonious structure, in which, with the manifold help of men's brains and hands, the process of affairs is fulfilled.
>
> Feelings are "within," where life is lived and man recovers from institutions.

> Here the spectrum of the emotions dances before the interested glance. Here a man's liking and hate and pleasure are indulged and his pain if it is not too severe. Here he is at home and stretches himself out in his rocking-chair. (Buber, 1958: 62–3)

This is inadequate as "the separated *It* of institutions is an animated clod without soul [a translation of the word 'golem'] and the separated *I* of feelings an uneasily-fluttering soul-bird" (Buber, 1958: 63). What is missing is the sense of a person: "institutions know only the specimen, feelings only the 'object'; neither knows the person, or mutual life" (Buber, 1958: 63). The move is from *individual* to *person*. Buber concludes his recorded conversation with the therapist Rogers, "if I may say expressly Yes and No to certain phenomena, I'm *against* individuals and *for* persons" (Buber, 1998: 174).

Buber and Macmurray both describe relations as at the heart of spirituality. We only know people through particular kinds of relationships and we only *are* people in and through our relationships. Knowing the person is an *action*, not a *state of mind* but a kind of *imaginative leap* to the reality of the other person. The action of knowing is therefore an act of *inclusion*: "It is inclusion – imagining the real [*Realphantasie*] – that banishes the illusion that we are confined to our skins or our own private experiences, as so many people think" (Friedman, 1999: 410, writing about Buber). We can be in dialogue, and dialogue is always an act of inclusion. Further, we can love, a particular act of inclusion.

> Love does not cling to the *I* in such a way as to have the *Thou* only for its "content," its object; but love is *between I* and *Thou*. The man who does not know this, with his very being know this, does not know love; even though he ascribes to it the feelings he lives through, experiences, enjoys and expresses. (Buber, 1958: 28–9)

As Shakespeare said, love is a "marriage of true minds" which "alters not with his brief hours and weeks, / But bears it out even to the edge of doom" (Sonnet 116). This is a religious obligation, according to Buber, and he links the Jewish and Christian approaches to love:

> To the question . . . which was the all-inclusive and fundamental commandment, the "great" commandment, Jesus replied by connecting the two Old Testament commandments between which above all the choice lay: "love God with all your might" and "love your neighbour as one like yourself". Both are to be "loved", God and the "neighbour" (i.e. not man in general, but the man who meets me time and again in the context of life), but in different

> ways. The neighbour is to be loved "as one like myself" (not "as I love myself"; in the last reality one does not love oneself, but one should rather learn to love oneself through love of one's neighbour), to whom, then, I should show love as I wish it may be shown to me. But God is to be loved with all my soul and all my might. By connecting the two Jesus brings to light the Old Testament truth that God and man are not rivals. (Buber, 2002: 60)

Overcoming Denial: Religious Education

In terms of RE, a single well-tried lesson can be described that illustrates how the philosophies of Buber and Macmurray might be enacted in schools. The lesson was originally developed by Marie Stern in a London special school (and reported variously in Stern, 1998; Stern, 2007: 162–3; and in detail in Stern, 2009a: 73–6), and it was used to help children with significant additional learning needs understand the number 6,000,000, as part of a course on the Shoah. In class, pupils are given a sheet with ten dots on it. Each dot was then labelled with the name and description of someone that pupil knew, either in school or at home. After the ten-dot sheet, a sheet was given with one hundred dots, and a similar exercise was completed, as a group. As there were just over a hundred pupils and staff at that school, it was possible to talk about all the people in the school: "this dot represents Karen in class three, and she is good at sport and music", and so on. A thousand-dot sheet, provided next, needed to restrict the information, with an arrow to individual dots labelled with the first name only of a person known to one of the pupils. And it was assumed that even if the whole class worked on a single sheet, it would be impossible to label every dot. Then an A4 sheet with 10,000 dots was used, made up of 100 blocks of 100 dots. (With adults, it is possible to start this lesson with the 10,000 dot sheet.) For this sheet, again, very brief labels are needed, perhaps just the initials of a person. Each group of pupils should start labelling dots, beginning at the top left hand corner. Even with a lot of preparation, pupils are unlikely to get beyond the first or second blocks of one hundred dots.

Once this work has been completed, the teacher should get the pupils to help roll out five rolls of paper, each roll consisting of 20 sheets of A3 paper with each sheet having six times 10 000 dots on it. (These dimensions have been carefully practised in many school settings.) The roll out (in a large classroom, or better still in a corridor or hall) will reveal exactly six million dots. This must only be done after the task of labelling: the pupils will understand large numbers, and will understand 6,000,000, in a way that they did not before. So will teachers. It may seem like a simple set of tasks, but it has touched many, many pupils and teachers, upset at the thought of the large number – whether it is applied to the Shoah, deaths in wars, or the analysis of poverty. Large numbers are worth knowing, personally; people are worth knowing, in large numbers. In a remarkably simple way, personal connections are expanded and given new meaning. The personal world of pupils is not only captured by the school: the school is able to set that in an historical context. By recognizing as individuals people who have died in such large numbers, the exercise can help pupils overcome the denial of death, and can help them recognize their closeness to the living. It is therefore a way of making *individuals* into *people*, and goes to the heart of engaging schooling, engaging RE: how can we treat people as ends in themselves and not means to ends?

Through a deep understanding of love and death, and an understanding of how that can be addressed in school RE, we can go some way to overcome the denials of death and of love. This will be achieved, according to Buber and Macmurray, through dialogue, an act of inclusion, in community. The *Spirit of the School* project has investigated how school communities work. It has involved empirical research in a number of schools in the UK and Hong Kong since 2006, and as a result of that work, alongside the philosophical investigation, the *spirited school* was defined in the following way: "The spirited school is an inclusive community with magnanimous leadership that enables friendship through dialogue in order to create and evaluate valuable or beautiful meanings, valuable or beautiful things, and good people" (Stern, 2009b: 161).

A longer version of that definition, with some added explanation, is this:

> The spirited school is an inclusive (bringing in from past times and local and distant places) community (people treating each other as ends in themselves) with magnanimous leadership (aiming for the good of the led) that enables (but does not insist on) friendship (by overcoming fear and loneliness and allowing for solitude) through dialogue (not monologue) in order to create and evaluate valuable or beautiful meanings, valuable or beautiful things (including the environment), and good (real) people. (Stern, 2009b: 160–1)

From those definitions, six questions were derived, to be asked of RE teachers. Responses to each of the questions would help explain how RE can overcome the denial of love and death, and can therefore promote dialogic learning communities. The questions ask

1 Who do you bring in to the school, in RE?

2 How do you treat people as ends in themselves, in RE?

3 In what ways are you magnanimous, in RE?
4 How do you enable friendship to thrive in RE?
5 Are you in dialogue, in RE?
6 How do you take part in creating meanings, things, and people, in RE?

These are the testing questions, and they are commended as ways of investigating how *engaging* is RE. The dots lesson, described above, is a helpful response to questions 1 and 2, and can help respond to question 4. Other case studies could be provided that help respond to other questions, and the examples given in Stern, 2007: 81–9, are starting points.

RE is a subject that draws on the cultures and ideas of peoples from around the world and from all times, and combines this interest with the personal cares and joys of the pupils themselves. The subject is therefore in a sense at the crossroads of the curriculum, the point at which all the present and personal aspects of schooling (also addressed by personal subjects such as personal and health education) meets all the historic and external aspects of schooling (also addressed by social science subject and the study of literature). It is a subject grounded in both the present and the past, the here and the there, the living and the dead. RE is therefore a *life-and-death* subject, or perhaps a *love-and-death* subject, at the heart of the curriculum.

Conclusion

Given the difficult subject matter of love and death, it is valuable complementing the case studies from schools by looking at what pupils say when surveyed more generally. In October 1997, as part of an RE festival, the professional body for UK Teachers of RE, the PCfRE (now NATRE) issued a questionnaire that was completed by over 16,000 young people in schools. Roughly 10% of the questionnaires were transcribed, and a smaller number were entered on an online database <www.pcfre.org.uk/db/>. There were also curriculum guides based on the questionnaire (Fageant and Blaylock, 1998; Weston, 2003). Question 3 on the survey asked the following:

> Here are two viewpoints about death: "When we die, we lie in the grave, and I'm afraid that's the end of us." "I think dying is like being born. You leave the place you know, but you go to a wonderful place you don't know." What are your thoughts about death and the afterlife?

Some of the 11-year-old respondents, who at this stage would have spent just a few weeks in their new secondary schools, expressed relatively conventional views that might have been drawn from RE, and external religious and humanist, learning. For example: "Death is not a nise [*sic*] feeling but when you go to heven [*sic*] in [*it*] will be like wonderful land." Or: "I think there isn't really a heaven. I think we just get buried and that's it, nothing else." However, the complexity, the depth of thought, and the personal engagement with the issues of many of the responses, all suggest that pupils are able to tackle some of the biggest questions. One child says with great eloquence:

> I think you die because you have been on earth for a while and now God wants you up there with him. Up where the sky's always blue, where you can never leave the ones you love and treasure.

Many children, religiously self-identified as Christian or as none, write about coming back or reincarnation. One child, identifying herself as Christian, says: "I think you could come back but as a spirit to help with good but I could feel something at my Grandmas house when my Grandad died and my dad can too." Another respondent (religiously described as none) says:

> I believe that when we die our body rots away, but our spirit (excluding) our memory) goes into a new born baby. However if the person has some unfinished work or business to take care of their spirit will try and correct it.

A more complex view, from a child who does not indicate her religion:

> I beleive that when you die, you do have an afterlife because i find that when you do die you go to a place eg: heaven and live an afterlife, not into another person but a living creature or plant. I have always thought that when my hamster died she was the tree I had planted on her grave. So I think there is an afterlife.

It is fear that comes through, however, as dominating a number of responses.

> I believe in afterlife but sometimes I am afraid of death. I think when people die they live in another world I think the criminals are still acepted by god becasue god will forgive everyone if you want be forgiven.

One of the most poignant of all the responses simply says "I afraid of death but part of me want's [*sic*] to die". It is difficult to see how the issues raised by these pupils could be discussed and built upon other than in RE.

RE has a special place in the curriculum as a subject able to tackle death, in ways that do not deny the real feelings and fears of pupils. Schools are hosting young people who have complex and powerful views, expressed in these examples by pupils who had just entered secondary schools and who were therefore unlikely to have been greatly influenced by the curriculum in their current schools. It is suggested that pupils have a right to a curriculum that actively engages with those views, and RE is put forward as a vehicle for such engagement. The engagement will of necessity be dialogic, not least because dialogue helps satisfy "the demand for fairness" (Smart, 1960: 13). Smart continues:

> The dialogue form also emphasizes anew the point that where there is discussion, there reasons are found. The possibility of argument implies that there are criteria of truth, however vague. Indeed, the man [*sic*] who refuses to argue at all is guilty of slaying truth: both the true and the false perish, and he is reduced to mere expressions of feeling. (Smart, 1960: 14)

Anne Tyler's novel *The Tin Can Tree* starts with a child's funeral. Later, a group of women discuss what to do about the child's mother. It is a long discussion. Finally, the character Missouri tells Joan: "Bravest thing about people, Miss Joan, is how they go on loving mortal beings after finding out there's such a thing as dying." After this exchange, Charleen says, "Was *that* what you did all this talking to say?" "It was," replies Missouri (Tyler, 1965: 76–7). May RE teachers be as brave, carrying on teaching about love alongside teaching about death.

References

Bradford, R. 2005. *First Boredom, Then Fear: The Life of Philip Larkin.* London. Peter Owen.

Buber, M. 1958. *I and Thou,* trans. Ronald Gregor Smith. 2nd ed. Edinburgh. T&T Clark.

Buber, M. 1998. *The Knowledge of Man: Selected Essays.* New York. Humanity Books.

Buber, M. 2002. *Between Man and Man.* London. Routledge.

Buruma, I., and Margalit, A. 2004. *Occidentalism: The West in the Eyes of Its Enemies.* London. Penguin.

Fageant, J., and Blaylock, L. (eds). 1998. *Faith in the Future: An Anthology of Pupils' Writing from the National RE Festival Questionnaire.* Birmingham. PCfRE.

Friedman, M. 1999. 'The Interhuman and What is Common to All: Martin Buber and Sociology', *Journal for the Theory of Social Behaviour* 29(4): 403–17.

Hull, J. M. 1998. *Utopian Whispers: Moral, Religious and Spiritual Values in*

Schools. Norwich. RMEP.
Jackson, R. 2004. *Rethinking Religious Education and Plurality: Issues in Diversity and Pedagogy.* London. RoutledgeFalmer.
Larkin, P. 1988. *Collected Poems,* ed. with an Introduction by Anthony Thwaite. London: The Marvell Press and Faber and Faber.
Long, E. T. 2000. *Twentieth-Century Western Philosophy of Religion 1900–2000.* Dordrecht, The Netherlands. Kluwer.
Macmurray, J. 1935. *Creative Society: A Study of the Relation of Christianity to Communism*. London. SCM Press.
Macmurray, J. 1968. *Lectures/Papers on Education.* Edinburgh: Edinburgh University Library, Special Collections Gen 2162/2.
Macmurray, J. 1979. *Ye Are My Friends and To Save From Fear.* London. Quaker Home Service.
Macmurray, J. 1992. *Freedom in the Modern World.* New Jersey. Humanities Press.
Macmurray, J. 1995. *Search for Reality in Religion.* London & Toronto. Quaker Home Service and the John Macmurray Society.
Macmurray, J. 1996. *The Personal World: John Macmurray on Self and Society* sel. and intro. Philip Conford. Edinburgh. Floris.
Peterson, C. 2006. *A Primer in Positive Psychology.* Oxford. Oxford University Press.
QCA. 2004. *Religious Education: the Non-Statutory National Framework.* London: Qualifications and Curriculum Authority.
Smart, N. 1960. *A Dialogue of Religions.* London. SCM Press.
Snyder, C. R., and Lopez, S. J. (eds). 2005. *Handbook of Positive Psychology.* Oxford. Oxford University Press.
Steiner, R. 1996. *Rudolf Steiner in the Waldorf School: Lectures and Addresses to Children, Parents, and Teachers – 1919–1924*. Hudson, NY. Anthroposophic Press.
Stern, L. J. 1998. *Three Steps to Heaven: Numeracy and RE.* Osterley. BFSS National RE Centre, Brunel University.
Stern, L. J. 2007. *Schools and Religions: Imagining the Real.* London. Continuum.
Stern, L. J. 2009a. *Getting the Buggers to Do Their Homework.* 2nd edn. London. Continuum.
Stern, L. J. 2009b. *The Spirit of the School.* London. Continuum.
Tyler, A. 1965. *The Tin Can Tree.* London. Vintage.
Weston, D. 2003. 'Children Talking Online', *RE Today* 21(1): 30–1.

Chapter Two

The Prevent Strategy and Consequences: Teaching of Jihad in RE Lessons

Heather Marshall

The aim of this paper is to begin to understand the government's Prevent Strategy, whose primary focus is the prevention of al-Qaeda influenced terrorism, looking at its implications for teachers and concentrating on strands specifically relating to local authority partners, including schools, and relating them to pedagogy and classroom practice. The Prevent Strategy identifies teaching about and building resilience to controversial issues as the key to prevention. In western countries, Islam is generally associated with al-Qaeda, terrorism, 9/11, 7/7, Palestine, the Iraq and Afghan invasions and Iran, and in western media "jihad" is used to refer to terrorist attacks organized by alleged militant fundamental Muslims. Such association and media coverage fuels fear and hatred, so the Prevent Strategy seemed the ideal base for this research. The first objective is to aid teachers in their understanding of the strategy; the second is to discover how Islam and more precisely jihad is taught in RE lessons, looking at the teacher perspective including teaching materials; and the third is to suggest and create a curriculum and pedagogy to begin to build resilience.

The Prevent Strategy

In May 2008 the government's Prevent Strategy added a local element to a global issue. Schools, identified as a tool for tackling extremist opinion and ideology, were now required to respond to this threat and play their part in the prevention of violent extremism, as well as creating a curriculum which deals with stereotyping and the increase in Islamophobia. This challenge and strategy sounds a number of alarms and raises a number of questions.

> This country, like many others, faces a challenge from terrorism and violent extremism. A very small minority seek to harm innocent people in the name of an ideology which causes division, hatred and violence. It is the role of government to take the tough security measures needed to keep people safe. But a security response alone is not enough; as with many other challenges,

a response led and driven by the community is also vital. (United Kingdom. HM Government, 2008: Ministerial Foreword)

Origins

In May 2008 HM Government produced *The Prevent Strategy: A Guide for Local Partners in England* with the subtitle *Stopping People Becoming or Supporting Terrorists and Violent Extremists*. The counter-signatures of the document show that the agenda has full governmental support from the top down. The Prevent Strategy is looking to community partners and partnerships to develop and implement effective action which will ultimately make the UK a safer place. The document focuses almost entirely on the threat of al-Qaeda influenced terrorism, explaining that a distorted interpretation of Islam, history, and politics is used to justify attacks against civilians both here and overseas.

To respond to this threat, the government developed a counter-terrorism strategy which came to be known as CONTEST (United Kingdom. HM Government, 2008). With four main components, the government were seen as taking tough security measures to keep people safe. These are:

Pursue – to stop terrorist attacks

Prepare – where we cannot stop an attack, to mitigate its impact

Protect – to strengthen our overall protection against terrorist attacks

Prevent – to stop people becoming terrorists or supporting violent extremists

(United Kingdom. HM Government, 2008: 5)

However, the CONTEST strategy was seen as being insufficient, and a longer term and broader programme, particularly around the area of Prevent, was thought to be needed. Believing that it is a combination of interlocking factors which causes violent extremism, the government was now seeing preventing extremism as a major long-term struggle, which needed to be addressed at various levels, including grass-roots and local levels. From these assessments and principles, the Prevent Strategy was created to guide local authorities and other partner agencies in taking this work forward.

Outline

The Prevent Strategy has five key threads and objectives for addressing the factors leading to people becoming or supporting violent extremism or terrorists, each playing a crucial part in the notion of prevention. The first of these threads, "challenging", holds that violent extremist ideology needs to be challenged, rather than simply ignored or rejected, and mainstream voices need to be exercised and heard to combat any ideology which could be considered extremist. The second, "disrupting", holds that the promotion of violent extremism and those individuals and institutions which seek to endorse it need to be disrupted and removed from their power positions. The third, "supporting", that susceptible and vulnerable individuals targeted and recruited by extremist individuals, groups, or institutions need to be supported in order to decrease the likelihood of them being drawn into extremist violence or ideology. The fourth, "increasing", that communities need to increase their resilience to violent extremism, and the last, "addressing", that grievances and issues which extremist ideologies exploit should be addressed and tackled.

This whole strategy, whilst driven by central government, relies on local communities to play an integral part, asking them to take a lead in establishing effective multi-agency planning to develop and deliver responses which are co-ordinated. The active participation of a range of partners is seen as crucial. Essentially, work on preventing violent extremism should embrace the experience, energy, and ideas of the whole community, and through active engagement the objectives of the strategy should be met.

"Learning Together to be Safe"

In October 2008 the DCSF (Department for Children, Schools and Families) published *Learning Together to be Safe: A Toolkit to Help Schools Contribute to the Prevention of Violent Extremism*. This stated that "schools can make an important contribution, being a focal point for local communities and helping to build mutual respect and understanding" (DCSF, 2008: 4). The toolkit takes the form of guidelines and suggestions about how schools can work with partner community organizations in work to tackle extremism. Recognizing the potential vulnerability of all school pupils to propaganda by extremist groups and also the positive influence that schools can be in the lives of pupils and the communities they serve, the toolkit is intended as guidance to help schools refocus to meet the objectives and new themes of the Prevent Strategy. The toolkit seeks to raise awareness of the threat and risks, provide information about the causes of extremism and about preventive action, help schools make a positive contribution to communities whilst protecting the well-being of pupils, and finally aid them in managing risks to the school community.

> In a school context the five strands are to:
>
> 1. Understand how an extremist **narrative** which can lead to harm can be challenged by staff in schools; and model to pupils how diverse views can be heard, analysed and challenged in a way which values freedom of speech and freedom from harm.
>
> 2. Understand how to **prevent harm** to pupils by individuals, groups or others who promote violent extremism, and manage risks within the school.
>
> 3. Understand how to **support individuals** who are vulnerable through strategies to support, challenge and protect.
>
> 4. Increase the **resilience of pupils and of school communities** through helping pupils acquire skills and knowledge to challenge extremist views, and promoting an ethos and values that promotes respect for others.
>
> 5. Use teaching styles and curriculum opportunities which allow **grievances** to be aired, explored and demonstrate the role of conflict resolution and active citizenship. (DCSF 2008: 7)

The toolkit recognizes the good practice and work that schools already do but also suggests that more should be done. Offering practical advice to schools in four areas – leadership and values; teaching, learning and the curriculum; pupil support processes; and managing risk and responding to events – schools are challenged to build on existing universal, targeted and specialist work and to develop it further in union with other local agencies and activities.

The crucial part of this agenda for teachers is the teaching, learning and curriculum area. The primary aim of this strand is the creation of a "curriculum and pedagogy which promote knowledge, skills and understanding to build the resilience of pupils and explore controversial issues" (DCSF, 2008: 9). In terms of grass-root teaching, this is the part of the strategy which will have the greatest influence. The main issue is being teaching and learning strategies which explore controversial issues in a way which promotes critical analysis and promotes shared values and visions. In this respect, the curriculum needs to be adapted to meet local needs, challenge extremist ideology, and promote universal rights as agreed by the UN. Although the toolkit looks to a variety of subjects, noting that history, geography, citizenship, and English all have a role to play, RE seems to have a greater responsibility, because "'the case for understanding religion could not be more powerful, for the very survival of civilization may depend on it" (Watson and Thompson, 2007: 17). The daily diet of newspaper and television reports about political conflict and terrorism relating to religion, and more specifically Islam, suggests that pupils need to be able to understand the vibrant and diverse beliefs of Muslims as well as learning about the doctrines, however controversial or hard these might be to teach. This is eloquently explained by Rowan Williams (2004): "the question is not so much why some Muslims are suicide bombers as why most aren't and couldn't conceive of being". To build the resilience of pupils, as one of the objectives of the toolkit, I agree with the Archbishop that RE curriculum and pedagogy should not shy away from controversial issues but should explore them directly, providing pupils with the knowledge, skills, and understanding to handle them.

Criticisms

Criticisms of the Prevent Strategy have come from many sides, not least from the Muslim community itself. The An-Nisa Society suggests that the government's strategy is "flawed and fraught with perils" (An-Nisa Society, 2009: 3). Their main criticisms are, first, that it has led to the disproportionate criminalization of Muslim communities, locating the burden for fighting terrorism on Muslim communities whilst neglecting to account for the majority peace-loving population. Secondly, its usage of terminology such as "violent extremism" ignores the very real threat from far-right and other extremist groups, reinforcing negative stereotypes and associations of Islam being synonymous with terrorism, thereby making the problem of terrorism a single issue relating to British Muslims. Finally, it actually dismantles traditional relationships of trust and confidence between public bodies and service users, through the "securitization" of Islam, leading to an abandonment of funding for traditional community development and replacing it with community cohesion, anti-extremist and anit-terrorist approaches, putting Muslim communities under an intense spotlight of the media and far-right groups. Making a number of recommendations, it calls for the strategy to be rethought, "to cease dealing with the whole Muslim community through the prism of anti-terrorism" (2009: 29) but to address issues of Islamphobia and the targeting of Muslims as a socially excluded group.

Even with the criticisms and failings outlined above, schools and teachers have a responsibility to tackle Islamophobia in lessons and to present Islam in a way that contradicts what the media often portray, as suggested by the European Union Monitoring Centre on Racism and Xenophobia:

> Muslims are often stereotypically portrayed in media reports as a devoutly religious and undifferentiated group sharing a fundamentalist version of Islam. This image conceals major differences in religious beliefs and practices resulting from Muslims' different national, cultural and religious backgrounds. It also conceals the fact that Muslim identities, especially among the younger generation, have undergone and are undergoing important transformations in response to developments both within and external to Muslim communities. (EUMC, 2006: 33)

Again, teachers, and more specially RE teachers, should be prepared to teach the very controversial issues that when decontextualized and misunderstood demonize Islam. More importantly in light of such criticism, there is a "need to express our solidarity with Muslims as fellow human beings by giving an alternative to the media images of Islam" (Smalley, 2005: 4). Classrooms should be the place to begin to tackle the issues raised by the An-Nisa Society as well as those proposed by the Prevent Strategy itself.

Controversial Issues

Stradling et al. (1984: 9) identify controversial issues as "those issues on which our society is clearly divided and significant groups within society advocate conflicting explanations or solutions based on alternative values". With many issues being classified as controversial, it is worth noting at this point that there is a difference between controversial and sensitive issues. As suggested in the Prevent Strategy, there is a link between building the resilience of pupils and tackling controversial issues in the classroom, and these do not need to be shocking or one dimensional, but do need to be faced up to and presented in an honest and confident manner. Allowing pupils to fully understand issues such as jihad, forced marriage, and the BNP allows those pupils to develop resilience to the potentially harmful, false ideologies, doctrines, and interpretations that exist. Controversy is part of living in modern society and follows not only adults but also children at every step as we try to make sense of what is acceptable in a democratic society. RE lessons provide excellent opportunities for pupils to explore current conflicts and controversies in greater depth. Developing the ability to talk and discuss with those of opposing views can be the best way of avoiding situations of conflict escalating into violence.

> Young people need the skills necessary to be able to sort fact from opinion, to be aware of their own values and the impact these have on their opinions, to research and listen before coming to a view, to be willing to change, to negotiate, discuss and represent others' opinions. (Wilkins, 2008)

I believe that pupils should explore how it is that individuals, even within the same culture, society, religion and so on, can apparently arrive at different perspectives on an issue. Introducing them to varied and multiple perspectives should therefore be a crucial part of the curriculum.

Teachers and controversy

Despite young people being regularly exposed to the conflicts and controversies of adult life, research indicates that one of the most common approaches adopted by teachers to the teaching of controversial issues is to avoid them completely. Peter Brett (2006) states that "youngsters are used to 'grazing' and 'gazing' without being always challenged to *really* look, engage and think". Teachers need to be proactive, ready to engage in debate themselves, being ready to challenge and be challenged. The success of the implementation of the Prevent Strategy will depend, in part, on how well prepared teachers are for teaching about controversial issues. As the Prevent Strategy focusses primarily on Islam and al-Qaeda, the teaching of jihad in RE seems to be the most obvious choice of controversial issue on which to base this research.

Jihad

> It is a commonplace that the way terrorist activities are reported results in a sense in most parts of the world that Islam and Muslims are engaged in a battle to take over the world and overthrow western civilization. Such reporting usually takes at face value the equation of jihad with terrorism and suicide bombing, and has got much worse since the events of 11 September 2001. (Smalley, 2005: 2)

Jihad, its teaching, and its portrayal in the media have become a controversial issue, an issue that many feel is easier to sidestep than to address directly. So why has jihad become such a controversial issue? Going back to Stradling's definition of the term "controversial", the notion of jihad and its definitions does divide groups. These groups vary and include the media, governments, teachers, and even sub-groups within the Muslim community itself. Explanations of jihad are conflicting, and much debate centres upon interpretations of the word and its true meaning, with alternative values being offered and solutions being based on different understandings. Smalley (2005) identifies the misconception of the term jihad and its equation with terrorism, a definition which is widely accepted within the Western world, despite many Islamic scholars vigorously challenging the legitimacy of violent extremist groups, which in itself is controversial. Furthermore, accepting that jihad is synonymous with violent extremism means that any discourse surrounding it becomes emotive, as many people have been affected by terrorism or perceive it as a genuine threat to civilization, making it especially controversial.

Ali (1983: 528) states that "great misconceptions prevail with regards to the duty of jihad in Islam". What is interesting and possibly unique about the controversy of teaching and discussing the notion of jihad is the fact it is perceived as being controversial within the community itself. Although for many scholars the essence of jihad is an internal struggle of the soul against it own negative forces, different interpretations still exist and are used as justification for atrocities, the Islamic Jihad Movement based in Palestine being an example. Hostility and a reluctance on the part of the Muslim community to engage in discussion and dialogue on this issue seems commonplace, adding to its controversy.

> The "triggers" of Islamism and violent jihad are not to be discovered in Islam or its theology but in the human agency manipulating and thus re-creating and re-inventing the "Islamic theologies" while it posits itself as being authentic and pristine. (Zemni, 2007)

Why is teaching about jihad important?

> The events of 9/11 and 7/7, the aftermath of Afghanistan and Iraq invasions, and terrorist attacks throughout the world have led to an increase in anti-Muslim sentiment, expression and action. (Coles, 2008: 13)

The popular media and their influence over modern society all too often misrepresent Islamic belief and practices, which in turn maintain myths, misrepresentation, and misunderstanding. This includes Muslims often being stereotyped as religious fanatics and terrorists posing a direct threat to the west. It is therefore imperative, in order to break these misconceptions, that teachers provide pupils with the complexities of the meaning of jihad and make them aware that definitions differ across cultures. James Moore writes:

> Defining jihad as a holy war and ignoring its other meanings, such as the inner struggle to achieve moral self-improvement, is not educationally sound; however, teaching students that complex terms have multiple meanings will enhance their understanding of Islam. (2006: 284)

The small scale research conducted for this project has indicated the bias towards defining jihad as a holy war, equating jihad with notions of violence, conflict, and terrorism. In order to combat the Islamophobia that is so prevalent, teachers have to both teach about jihad and be certain to present it in an educationally sound way, including the different definitions and understandings. Negative experiences of Islam and Muslims are compounded by the media, and this makes Islam and specifically jihad particularly difficult to teach. Nevertheless, the importance of doing so is clear. Returning to the primary aim of the teaching, learning, and curriculum area of the teachers' toolkit, teaching the true nature of jihad and its exploration, regardless of its controversies, is essential in promoting knowledge, skills, and understanding to build the resilience of pupils to negative stereotypes, doctrine, understanding, and so on. It is important that teachers deal directly with controversial issues, as avoidance only exacerbates the inevitable confusion.

Current jihad teaching

Resources

A review of current RE textbooks, resources and support materials has revealed that responsibility for misconceptions and controversy about jihad does not just lie with the media but also with educators. At KS3, many of the resources included the topic of jihad in topics such as war, fighting, and terrorism, the concept of "holy war" being referred to on numerous occasions. Some do make an attempt to distinguish between lesser and greater jihad, but the lesser is commonly more explicit. The Qur'an is frequently referred to but again this is often to support lesser jihad and the notion of defending or fighting for Islam. Some choose to include Muslim commentary which offers alternative explanations and clarity to the widespread understanding, playing up the greater and more personal struggle. Tasks include getting pupils to list the advantages and disadvantages of jihad, to reflect upon a quote from the Qur'an, but often they would again relate to holy war and the idea of crusade and whether this is justified.

GCSE specifications were also scrutinized, and similar issues to those at KS3 became quickly apparent. Within the topics, jihad was slotted into such areas as "attitudes to war", "Muslim just war theory" and "religion and conflict". Terms used to describe jihad included terrorism, holy war, conflict, faith and sanctity of life, with the implication that exam boards seem to want to emphasize the notion of lesser jihad. OCR include jihad in their "core beliefs" section in its Islam specification being careful to differentiate between greater and lesser (www.ocr.org.uk), and Edexcel place it in "living the Muslim life", again within its Islam paper, looking at the effects it has on the lives of Muslims, but these examples are few and far between even within newly revised specifications (www.edexcel.com). It is interesting that both the KS3 and KS4 resources focus on the more controversial lesser jihad.

Teachers

The next piece of research involved asking RE teachers[1] what they did in the classroom. A questionnaire was sent to approximately 40 teachers, its objective being to discover how teachers tackle the issue of jihad. Most respondents said that Islam is taught in RE lessons, but when taught at KS3 only a handful taught about jihad specifically, and even fewer made the distinction between lesser and greater jihad and felt confident that their pupils could make this distinction. The themes it occurred in most frequently were general Islam and religion in the media. At KS4, with many schools doing either short or full course GCSE, teaching was in line with the specifications and, depending on what board they opted for, jihad was covered in a variety of different ways. Again it occurs predominantly in the theme of war and peace, and a number of teachers did state that they try to tackle the misunderstanding of the term but still did not feel confident that pupils could distinguish or explain the idea of greater jihad. There seems to be a particular problem within faith schools, when very little multi-faith teaching occurs, with one respondent identifying the weakness of the Icons schemes of work and its limited reference to Islam and complete neglect of jihad.

All participants identified a weakness in the teaching of jihad, whether in their own school or as a collective problem, whilst recognizing the significance of teaching it correctly and not sidestepping it. One of the teachers stated: "personally I believe it is important to dispel widely held misunderstanding and any associated prejudice to support a more tolerant attitude within pupils", though interestingly his school did not teach about jihad despite his views. Respondents did however say that they did or would feel confident teaching jihad, despite its controversies.

Trainee teachers

The final piece of research involved current Secondary RE initial teacher trainees.[2] As the next generation of RE teachers, their understanding of jihad, their opinions of it, and their confidence in tackling it seemed crucial. Only 20% of respondents were actually taught about Islam whilst at school, so many struggled to make a distinction between lesser and greater jihad, with a general understanding of the term being struggle or holy war. Pupils from traditional Christian faith backgrounds found defining jihad the most difficult, possibly due to a lack of coverage in their own RE background. When asked what concepts jihad should be taught in, "terrorism", "conflict" and "just war" were the most commonly identified. One respondent wrote: "Conflict: to define and help develop an understanding of an overused phrase in the media." It is apparent that this group recognize the need for challenging pupils over their misconceptions of the term and the media portrayal of the concept, although many stated that they would feel uncomfortable teaching it without sufficient help and support. Many of the respondents expressed a concern about teaching jihad and presenting it in the correct way, using words like "sensitively" and "objectively", wanting to tackle misunderstanding but being uncertain of the concept themselves.

All respondents felt that teaching about jihad was either important or very important, the words "misunderstanding" and "misconceptions" being used often as a motivation and reasoning for this. Trainees are acutely aware of the controversies surrounding the concept of jihad, including its definition, the emotions it invokes, the misconceptions and stereotypes that exist around it, and its place in the curriculum, noting a lack of support and knowledge in this area as a big factor in this, but also see its importance, its relevance, and the significance of getting it right.

From this research it became apparent that the key to building pupil resilience was through increasing the confidence of teachers in pedagogy and teaching strategies, as well as the production of accurate and true resources.

Teaching Strategies

Many scholars, academics and teachers agree that religious education should reflect current needs and interests, for example building resilience, making responsible citizens and so on, of pupils and the wider society, and in successful lessons teachers should use their expert skills to encourage pupils to express themselves clearly, to give reasons and to think more deeply. Imran Ogra and Fatima Khan write:

> Good RE might aspire to go beyond this, so that children and young people learn more, and learn to reflect more deeply on the relevance and meaning of Islam as a way of life in RE lessons. We hope RE might lead young people to be confident in addressing the challenge of Islamophobia in society. (2004: 46)

Good RE

The role of RE has shifted over the past few decades, and the SCAA (1994) model syllabus for RE states that the subject should help pupils to "develop positive attitudes towards other people, respecting their right to hold different beliefs from their own, and towards living in a society of diverse religions". This commonly held view is what is most frequently promoted within RE classrooms; however, when it comes to the Prevent Strategy, teaching about controversial issues and jihad, this needs to go one step further. RE should look beyond simply promoting tolerance, but actually encourage positive and affirming relationships between people of different cultures and religions, so that misunderstanding and misconceptions, an example of which is the stereotyping of Muslims as terrorists, have a chance of being exposed. Religion should not be presented as monolithic but as varied; its greatest achievements as well as its most ferocious and evil ones should be presented. Pupils must learn about the rich and varied texture of Muslim people, moving away from a heavy reliance on doctrine and practices, often the primary focus of agreed syllabuses and schemes of work. The concept of learning *from* religion is crucial here, and includes a reflection on meaning and an application to pupils' own situations. A good example of this is the concept of "inner struggles" which relates to jihad and is easy for pupils to relate to.

The disagreements amongst both Islamic and non-Muslim scholars lead to confusion over the true ideas, the predominant belief of Islam, which in turn deters teachers from teaching these important, albeit seemingly controversial, topics. To aid with this, RE teachers must ensure that they exercize sound judgement when selecting resources and creating lesson plans, whilst being aware of the preconceptions included in textbooks and other resources. Pupils should be learning from examples which clearly contest commonly held stereotypes, as this is an excellent means of reducing prejudice and discrimination. Teachers can never teach from a perspective which is devoid of presupposition, so in order to balance this, educators must endeavour to present multiple perspectives. For example, for the complex and varied meanings behind the term "jihad", a varied and balanced approach will help to dispel stereotypes and misconceptions. Smalley (2005: 4), recognizing the need for pupils to be exposed to a range of views, opinions, choices, and so on, comments: "we are beginning to hear a multiplicity of voices in the media, so let's make sure we get them in our classrooms".

"The real issue is interpretation, in this case of Islam and the Qur'an," argue Watson and Thompson (2007: 149); with damage being caused, as Karen Armstrong points out, by "concentrating obsessively on the more aggressive verses of the Qur'an without fully appreciating how these are qualified by the text as a whole" (Armstrong, 2005: 25). It is therefore vital that a fair and true reading is taught. Teachers should not be reluctant to use original texts and primary sources, as this allows the Muslim voice to articulate the essentials of Islam. In the case of jihad it is undeniable that terrorists derive inspiration and cite the Qur'an as justification, so the challenge for educators is to offer alternative meanings.

A simplified and stereotypical view of jihad as "greater" jihad, and the ambiguities and controversy involved in this, means that teachers and pupils may not feel empowered to understand the radical Islamic narrative, certainly not empowered to prevent it; nor up-skilled enough to develop resilience or allow grievances to be aired. Radicals (both Islamic and far-right) might even wish to portray the emphasis upon the greater jihad as part of an establishment, naive and apologetic approach to Islam that, whilst well intentioned, nevertheless glosses over uncomfortable elements of the historical and present reality of jihad. This in turn could be seen as fuelling rather than confronting the radical agenda and its appeal to marginalized young people.

Practical suggestions

Philosophy for Children (P4C)

P4C is a philosophical approach based on the Socratic method, a moral and intellectual discipline founded on reason with a focus on giving the learner questions and not simple answers; its basis is in encouraging individuals to inquire about questions of interest and to deepen their ability to think, through the probing of the nature of a question or subject, inquiring about the data or information and considering alternative interpretations. Lipman, the creator of P4C, stated its aim as "not to change children's beliefs but to help them find better and more sufficient reasons for believing those things they chose to believe in" (1992: 26). Telling or preaching at young people about what to think is likely at best to have no effect and at worst to close their minds to alternative views. P4C allows pupils to expand their listening skills and respect for others' positions, through encouraging them to listen to the ideas of others, reflect on their viewpoints, and then present them publicly and also to alter their views in response to what they hear. A "conversation" develops from this methodology which provides a tool for engaging pupils at a much deeper level. The goal is to expand understanding rather than to emphasize memorization, through the application of knowledge, its investigation, synthesis, and assessment.

When teaching about a controversial area such as jihad, didactic approaches are not always suitable, as they touch on deeply held views and embedded attitudes. P4C offers:

> a demonstration of thinking that is caring (each member is supported and allowed to be an integral member of the community), creative (new ideas are sought out and encouraged) and critical (good responses are expected for one's ideas and positions. (Turgeon)

The aim of this is to create better thinkers, with a hope that they will become more caring members of society who can cope with differences at the same time as submitting differences to reasonable analysis. Black and Wiliam (2001) note the importance of a teacher moving from being one who presents facts to one who explores the pupils' ideas and brings them into the investigation until they learn the information that is required. The pupil is also moving, from being a passive observer, a sponge soaking up knowledge, to one who knows that learning depends on an ability to express, discuss, and explain ideas. Ultimately this encourages pupils to overwrite their misconceptions, misunderstandings, stereotypes, or wrong ideas with what the teacher knows to be true, promoting knowledge, skills, and understanding to build the resilience of pupils to negative stereotypes, doctrine, and understanding, aligned with the Prevent Strategy and also equipping them with the tools to challenge Islamophobia. Used in conjunction with the following ideas, P4C could prove very effective. (See the appendix for examples of using P4C in teaching about jihad.)

Thinking skills activities

Thinking skills activities such as diamond ranking, mysteries, and values continuums help develop reasoned arguments, as well as the organization of ideas as pupils sort, organize, and analyse large amounts of information. Through the examination of their own and other people's values and attitudes, their own critical thinking and reasoning skills are increased. (For examples of how this can be achieved when teaching the idea of greater jihad through the notion of inner struggles, see Figure 2-1 and the appendix at the end of this chapter.)

Visual stimuli

Visual stimuli, such as photographs or television news reports, encourage pupils to ask questions and explore bias, whilst developing analytical, inquiry, and critical thinking skills. They are a good basis for generating individual reflection, class and small group discussion, as pupils with varying levels of knowledge of a subject can respond to the same material. It also helps pupils to explore the different personal feelings and political reactions from cultures and countries different from their own. An example in relation to the teaching of jihad could be to use newspaper front pages following terrorist attacks to stimulate thinking and reflection, or television news reports to help pupils to understand the bias in reporting. (See appendix for more examples.)

Primary sources

It is vital that true and fair readings of primary sources are taught, but this does not refer exclusively to the Qur'an. Using sources such a biographies,

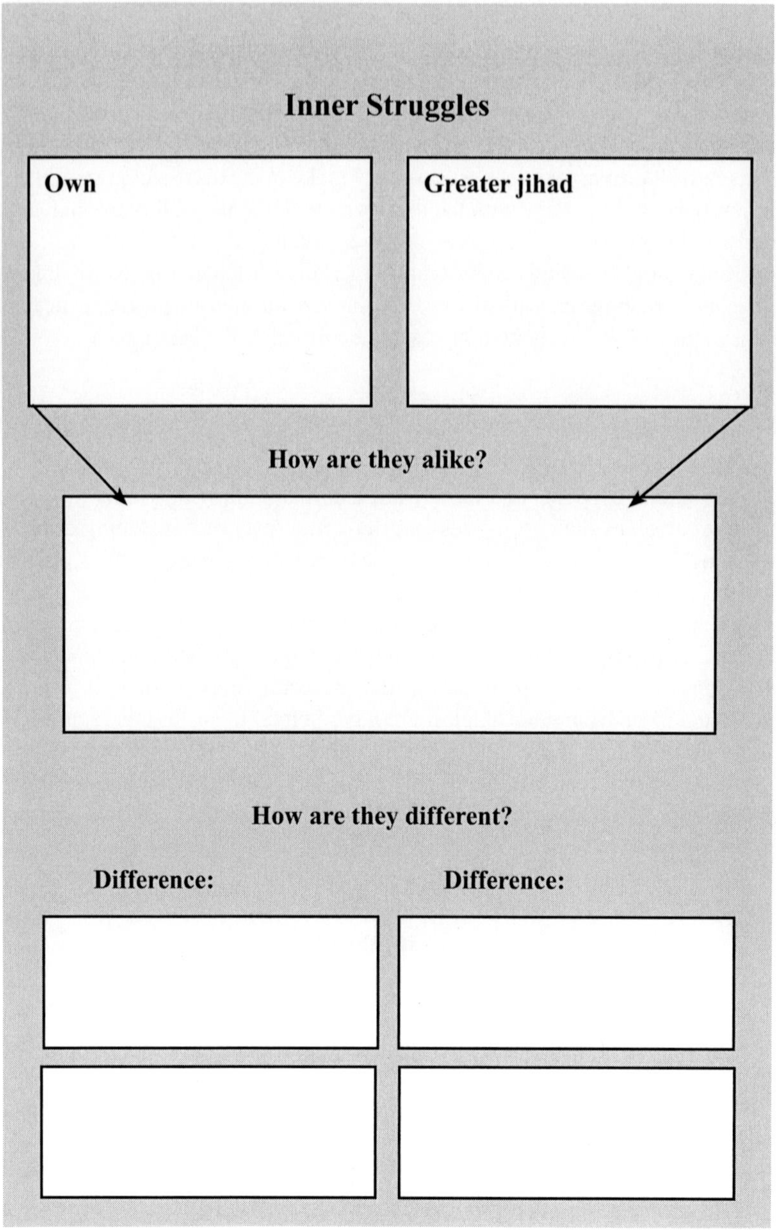
Inner Struggles
Own
Greater jihad
How are they alike?
How are they different?
Difference:
Difference:

Fig. 2-1

poetry, stories, and articles written by Muslims, for example to explain the ideas behind the notion of jihad, allows the ordinary or alternative voice to be heard. As stimuli, these can evoke a deeper level of reflection and discussion, especially if they challenge a misconception and allow pupils to grapple with their own suppositions. Julian Stern comments on the fear of RE teachers to engage with primary sources, in case they make mistakes or get it wrong. "It is surely better to engage with the text, even with the possibility of inadvertently making mistakes, than to avoid all engagement" (Stern, 2006: 15). An example could be using the biography of Badshah Khan "the Non-Violent of Islam" to show how jihad can be achieved through non-violent means. (Easwaran, 1999. Further examples can be found in the appendix.)

Learning from Islam

Using beliefs, concepts and ideas from Islam and allowing pupils to apply these to areas of their own lives is an effective way of developing critical thinking and resilience. Through the use of reasoning and examples, pupils can be encouraged for example to draw parallels between the inner struggles (jihad) faced by Muslims and those faced by themselves. Through this critical evaluation of Islamic teachings and their application, pupils are subsequently able to explain and justify an example of a situation or time when the ideas of greater jihad might have helped them. In this regard RE is about more than just the acquisition of knowledge; it builds understanding and empathy which fulfils its true purpose, a starting point being "What would it be like if this was happening to you?" or "How can this be applied to your own lives?"

Conclusion

The creation of a "curriculum and pedagogy which promote knowledge, skills and understanding to build the resilience of pupils and explore controversial issues" (DCSF, 2008: 9) is an incredibly important challenge. James Moore suggests that "education remains a potent tool in the struggle to balance vital national identity and security concerns with tolerance for religions, cultural and political diversity" (2006: 285). With this in mind, I have developed three separate lessons devoted to the teaching of jihad and more specifically "greater" jihad. Using the pedagogical recommendations of the Prevent Strategy and teachers' toolkit, alongside the research into

RE teachers, lessons and resources, these lessons have been produced with the aim of promoting knowledge, skills and understanding which will both endow teachers with the confidence to tackle this controversial area and ultimately build pupil resilience. This resilience should equip individuals to tackle Islamophobia, challenge extremist ideology, dispute media stereotypes, and refute fanatical doctrine.

I am acutely aware that the distinction between greater and lesser jihad is itself problematic within Islam, and that clearly defining the distinction between greater and lesser jihad is not in itself sufficient to address those five categories of the Prevent agenda. Nevertheless it can be a useful, and more immediate and accessible, starting point within the RE context and the limitations of curriculum time and subject knowledge training, hence the development of my scheme of work and resources. However, teachers must be aware that the issue goes a lot deeper and that extremists have very articulate and cogent arguments that seek to ground jihad firmly in historical, Islamic traditions of both Qur'anic exegesis and the sunna of Prophet Muhammad. If teachers and students are not aware of this, and think that to combat violent extremism it's just a matter of "enlightening" their pupils about the difference between greater and lesser jihad, the danger is that they, and maybe even their moderate Muslim students, are even more vulnerable to the rhetoric of extremists, including those far-right extremists who seek to claim that they are the ones facing up to and confronting the more troublesome realities of jihad.

Appendix: Examples from the Work Scheme

Lesson 1: Greater jihad – the inner struggle

Learning Objectives	Activities	Learning Outcomes	Resources
	STARTER: • Thunks: beguiling questions about everyday things that stop you in your tracks and help you start to look at the world in a new light. Can be discussed as a class or small group or reflected on individually. • Choose a thunk, or create your own.	To begin to think philosophically	Starter sheet 1
Appreciate the meaning of the word ‘struggle’	DISCUSSION: Write on the board: ‘What does struggle mean?’ Pupils (in groups of about four) begin to discuss and answer this question. • Each group to create their own definition of the word • Class discussion to conclude – beginning with small group definitions	Working definition of the word ‘struggle’	

Learning Objectives	Activities	Learning Outcomes	Resources
Think deeply about life struggles and their effects Effective group and discussion work Begin to understand that humans struggle with similar things	**MAIN ACTIVITY:** SNAKES AND LADDERS BOARD • Explain the symbolism and origin of the game: ladders represent the things that move people 'up' in life and snakes are the things people struggle with and so move them 'down' in life • All Muslims try hard to be close to God through the five pillars etc., but there are difficult feelings, emotions etc. in life that prevent this • Eight struggles: jealousy, greed, selfishness, anger, hatred, shame, agression and bitterness. Ensure pupils understand these terms. • Small groups: pupils to assign each struggle to a snake: the longer the snake the more difficult the struggle. • Pupils need to be able to explain why they have assigned the struggles to certain snakes. • Class discussion – feedback from task: longest and shortest snakes and why.	Identify key struggles Understand that belief and actions are linked Reflect on greater and lesser struggles	Snakes and ladders board Struggle cards

Learning Objectives	Activities	Learning Outcomes	Resources
To develop a greater understanding of the notion of jihad Begin to make the distinction between lesser and greater jihad	**GREATER JIHAD:** • Definition: 'Jihad is Arabic for effort and challenge; it is used to describe the personal struggle of each Muslim against the inner things that prevent them from getting close to Allah.' • Display this definition. How does this relate to the struggles they have been discussing? How would these prevent a Muslim from getting close to Allah? What are the similarities and differences between the struggles form the board and greater jihad?	Know the relationship between greater jihad and the concept of inner struggle	Definition
Reflect on own inner struggles Identification of the similarities and differences	**CONTRAST FRAME:** • Pupils to choose their own personal struggle or one from the snakes and ladders board; this is written into the 'Me' box, then the definition of greater jihad in the 'Jihad' box • Individually reflecting on the similiarities between them, complete the 'How are they alike?' box. Then 'How are they different?', noting two differences.	Relate the idea of struggle to greater jihad	Contrast frame

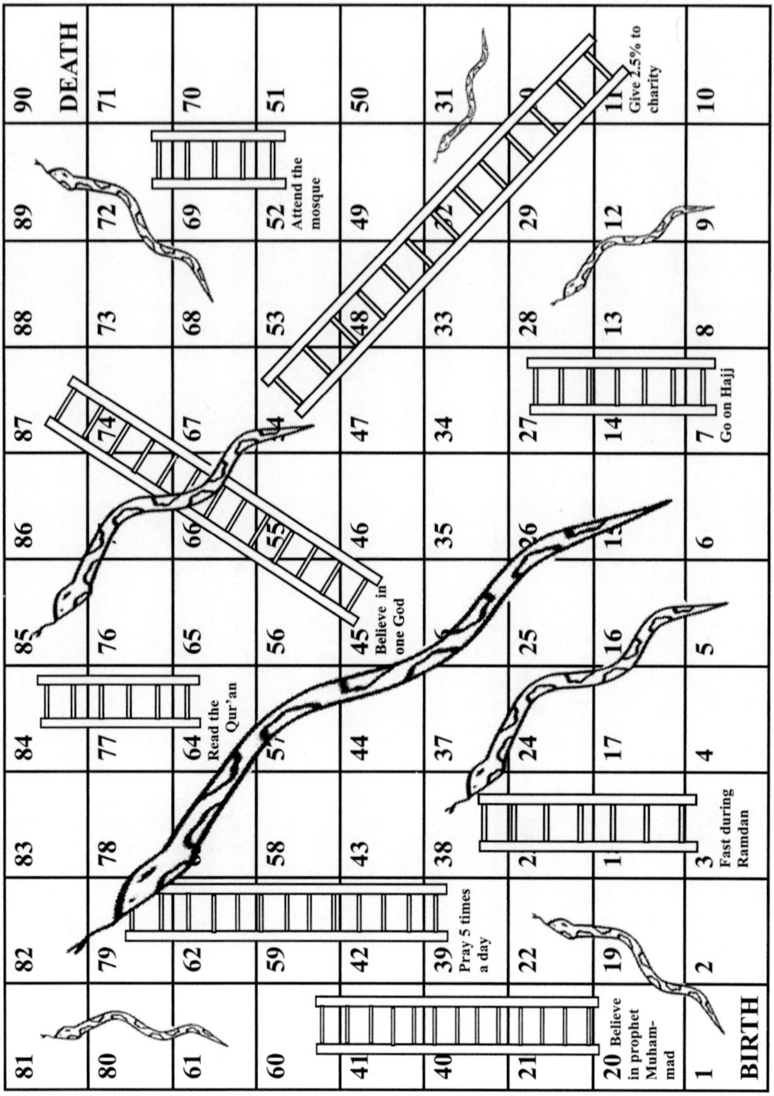

Fig. 2-2 Snakes and Ladders board

Lesson 3: Jihad and the media

Learning Objectives	Activities	Learning Outcomes	Resources
	Starter: • Thunks: beguiling questions about everyday things that stop you in your tracks and help you start to look at the world in a new light. Can be discussed as a class or small group or reflected on individually. • Choose a thunk, or create your own.	To begin to think philosophically	Starter sheet 1
Begin to reflect on where their ideas about jihad originate Understand the difference between lesser and greater jihad, and the implications of this	**Jihad Definition:** • Ask pupils for their ideas of jihad. Where do these come from? • General jihad definition: > 'Personal individual struggle against evil in the way of Allah. It can also be collective defence of the Muslim community.' • Make distinction between lesser and greater jihad. > Definition of greater jihad: 'the personal fight of each Muslim against the inner things that prevent them from getting close to Allah' > Definition of lesser jihad: 'the collective defence of the Muslim community' • Discuss the terms 'lesser' and 'greater'. Get pupils to think about which one is the more important to Muslims, noting the following: > Greater – 'personal struggle' > Lesser – 'collective defence'	Reflect on the ideas of lesser and greater Have a solid understanding of greater jihad and its importance	Definition

Learning Objectives	Activities	Learning Outcomes	Resources
Reflection on media influence. Begin to understand the media control over ideas and opinions Begin to develop ideas to solve the media issue Develop a good understanding of greater jihad.	**Main Activity:** News clip: Islamic terrorism? • Show pupils the following clips: > http://www.youtube.com/watch?v=Rfx4glTU5JQ > http://www.youtube.com/watch?v=045d0EUG_bQ > http://www.youtube.com/watch?v=xA6wu3UxT8c > http://www.youtube.com/watch?v=8efm9ThmsNE Follow up with brief discussion on how the media portray Islam and jihad. • In small groups, read articles and look at pictures. Discuss the messages of the media about Islam/Muslims. Are they fair and accurate, or biased? Why? • Pupils write down their ideas and be ready to discuss them with the class. • Thinking about the definition of jihad, do pupils htink it is fair of the media to keep using the word 'jihad' as justification? Which type of jihad do these reports, articles and pictures focus on? Why? • Pupils select four or five different pictures that show the protection/physical element of jihad, explaining why these have been selected.	Identify examples of media bias and control Relate their understanding to the influence of the media Understand how the media have distorted the understanding of jihad Offer solutions to the problems identified	News video Newspaper articles Photos Problem solver sheet Qur'an quotes sheet
	Problem Solver: • Pupils complete a sheet using one of the stimuli from the main activity.		Definition
	Good Jihad? • Small groups: discussion of 'What is jihad? What is good jihad?' • Use quotations form the Qur'an to back up arguments. • Discussion of ideas to close.		Contrast frame

Greater Jihad Qur'an Quotes Sheet

2:256 – There shall be no pressure in religion: the right way is now very different from the wrong way. Anyone who criticises the devil and believes in Allah has the strongest of bonds; one that never breaks.

47:7 – O you who believe, if you support GOD, He will support you, and strengthen your grip.

8:61 – If the enemy wants peace, you should also want peace, and trust in Allah: for He is the One that hears and knows all things.

16:125 – You shall show the way of your Lord through your wisdom and kindness, and debate with them in the best possible manner.

2:177 – It is correct to believe in Allah, the Last Day, the Angels, the Book and the Messengers; to give, out of love for Him, to your family, orphans, the needy, the vagrant and those who ask. It is also correct to be strong in prayer and practise regular charity.

2:187 – Does Allah not make clear His Signs to men; so that they may learn self-restraint?

41:34 – Goodness and Evil cannot be equal. Resist evil with what is better: Then the between whom and you was hatred will become good friends.

The Media Portrayal of Jihad – Problem Solver

1 What is the problem?

2 What information do we have to support this problem?

3 How good is the information/evidence?

4 What are the pros and cons of each alternative portrayal?

5 Which is the best alternative and why?

Notes

1 A group of 40 Liverpool secondary RE teachers were given a semi-structured questionnaire, these teachers were chosen at random from a local network group but care was taken to ensure that they represented different types of schools including faith institutions. The questionnaire focused on the teaching of Islam and asked about the place of jihad within this, asking teachers to explain where in the RE curriculum this appears, their attitude to teaching it and any challenges it raises.

2 A group of 40 secondary RE PGCE students completed a semi-structured questionnaire designed to ascertain their own knowledge of Islam, their attitude towards teaching it and to identify any challenges within doing so. The group were a mix of ages, abilities, ethnicities, and genders, all of them currently studying at Liverpool Hope University.

References

Ali, M.M. 1983. *The Religion of Islam.* Lahore. The Ahmadiyya Anjuman Isha'at Islam.

An-Nisa Society. 2009. *Preventing Violent Extremism (PVE) & PREVENT: A Response from the Muslim Community.* London. An-Nisa Society.

Armstrong, Karen. 2005. 'Unholy Scriptures', *The Guardian*, 11 August: 25.

Black, P., and Wiliam, D. 2001. *Inside the Black Box: Raising Standards through Classroom Assessment.* http://weaeducation.typepad.co.uk/files/blackbox-1.pdf. Accessed 27 October 2009.

Brett, P. 2006. Approaches to Teaching Controversial Issues. http://www.citized.info/pdf/conferences/31_03_06report.pdf. Accessed 27 October 2009.

Coles, M. 2008. Every Muslim Child Matters: Practical Guidance for Schools and Children's Services. Stoke-on-Trent. Trentham Books.

DCSF. 2008. *Learning Together to be Safe: A Toolkit to Help Schools Contribute to the Prevention of Violent Extremism.* Nottingham: Department for Children, Schools and Families.

Easwaran, E. 1999. *Nonviolent Soldier of Islam: Badshah Khan: A Man to Match his Mountains.* London. Nilgiri Press.

EUMC. 2006. *Muslims in the European Union – Discrimination and Islamophobia*, Brussels. EUMC Publications.

Khan-Cheema, M.A. 1994. 'British Muslims and the Maintained Schools', in Ashraf, S.A., and Hirst, P.A. (eds). *Religion and Education: Islamic and Christian Approaches.* Cambridge. Islamic Academy: 177–198.

Lipman, M. 1992. *Thinking in Education.* Cambridge: Cambridge University Press.

Moore, J. 2006. 'Teaching about Islam in Secondary Schools: Curricular and Pedagogical Considerations', *Equity & Excellence in Education*, 39(3): 279–286.

Moore, J. 2009. 'Why Religious Education Matters: The Role of Islam in Multicultural Education', *Multicultural Perspectives,* 11(3): 139–145.

Ogra, I., and Khan, F. 2004. *Helping Teachers Tackle My Religion in the Classroom: Guidance from Inside the Muslim Faith.* Birmingham. PcfRE.

SCAA. 1994. *Model Syllabuses for Religious Education, Model 1: Living Faiths Today.* London: School Curriculum and Assessment Authority.

Smalley, S. 2005. 'Teaching about Islam and Learning about Muslims: Islamophobia in the Classroom', *RE:Source*, 27(3): 4–7.

Stern, J. 2006. *Teaching Religious Education.* London. Continuum.

Stradling, R., et al. 1984. *Teaching Controversial Issues.* Teaching Matters. London. Hodder Arnold.

Turgeon, W. 'Metaphysical Horizons of Philosophy for Children', http://www.bu.edu/wcp/Papers/Chil/ChilTurg.htm. Accessed 27 October 2009.

United Kingdom. HM Government. 2008. *The Prevent Strategy: A Guide for Local Partners in England: Stopping People Becoming or Supporting Terrorists and Violent Extremists.* London. HM Government.

United Kingdom. HM Government. 2008. *The United Kingdom's Strategy for Countering International Terrorism.* Norwich. TSO.

Watson, B., and Thompson, P. 2007. *The Effective Teaching of Religious Education.* 2nd ed. London. Pearson.

Wilkins, A. 2008. *Controversy in Citizenship is Inevitable.* http://www.excellencegateway.org.uk/media/post16/files/controversialissued.pdf. Accessed 27 October 2009.

Williams, R. 2004. *Belief, Unbelief and Religious Education.* http://www.archibshopofyork.org/1173. Accessed 27 October 2009.

Zemni, S. 2007. *The West, Islam, Islamism and Jihad: Undigested Modernity and the Promise of Politics.* http://www.strategicforesight.com/iwforum/sami_zemini.htm. Accessed 27 October 2009.

Chapter Three

Creating and Engaging in Shared Space with Many Voices: Moving towards Constructive Community Dialogue in Oldham

Robert Thorne

History, Shared Space and Engagement

Trying to encourage positive engagement between people of different ethnic, religious and socio-economic backgrounds is one of the most pressing issues of the 21st century. The lack of mutually enriching engagement between such groups was brought into sharp focus through the civil disturbances in Oldham in May 2001. The challenges posed by this event and the fallout from it were summarized and succinctly expressed by Father Phil Sumner who leads Oldham Interfaith Forum:

> Oldham is regarded as the most segregated town in the country and when you've got that segregation you've got major problems. Engagement isn't happening on every street corner but it is happening. Things have got better. When I arrived many people in my own community said we don't speak to "them" [Muslims]. People are now saying we're speaking to them much more, but it is still "them"[1]

Against this regional backdrop, Oldham Sixth Form College (OSFC) has introduced a number of initiatives to promote engagement and community cohesion within and outside the college setting, in order to promote understanding, tolerance and integration between the different racial and religious constituents within the town. The college is a purpose built sixth form college in the centre of Oldham. Oldham has a population of 219,600 and is projected to grow by 4% reaching around 228,100 people in 2022. Relative deprivation has increased in the borough between the 2004 and 2007 Indices of Deprivation, with the biggest deterioration in relative position being on the income scale. Oldham is now ranked as the 42nd most deprived local authority in the country.

On 1 October 2008, the college had enrolled 2230 (full-time equivalent) learners aged 16 to 19, which is 35 FTE students above target. This figure in 2006/7 had been 2195. The large majority of these learners are following advanced level programmes. The college offers an extensive range of A2, AS and vocational courses at level 3. A smaller range of GCSE and vocational courses are offered at level 2. The level 2 offer is being reviewed for 2009/10. The college offered programmes in 12 of the 15 subject sector categories in 2007/8.

Learners come from the 11 partner schools in Oldham and also from across Greater Manchester and, in a small number of cases, from Yorkshire. In 2007/8, learners were recruited from 50 different institutions with 743 learners coming from the college's partner schools, an increase of 23 on 2006/7, and only the second time the college has recruited over 700 students from its 11 partner schools. A total 35% of learners were from an Asian heritage backgrounds and 39% from an ethnic minority backgrounds, as opposed to a local British and ethnic minority population of just under 20%. Some 57% of learners were female. In 2008/9 learners have been recruited from at least 46 separate institutions with 816 coming from the college's partner schools, a significant growth. A total of 37% of the student body is from an Asian heritage background and 41% from an ethnic minority background. Some 56% are female.

In March 2005, the college was awarded the Learning and Skills Beacon status by the Department for Education and Skills as a public recognition of its important work.

The college's mission is "to provide the highest quality education for students in Oldham and the local area so that they are equipped to the very best of their abilities to move into Higher Education or employment" – something staff are always working to achieve.

But the significant track record and statistics achieved by Oldham Sixth Form College only illustrate part of the institution's success. In order to address the needs and maximize the potential of the students in the town itself, it was decided that the college needed to be central to the educational life Oldham in real ways. A brave decision was taken to establish a new college in the centre of the town so that the educational rhetoric was worked out in practice. Many critics of this radical policy shift in the town greeted the decision with emotions ranging from scepticism to open hostility.

The college's detractors thought that it was reckless to place a state of the art facility in the heart of a depressed industrial town, many areas of which belied the title "King Cotton" that Oldham had been given in its heyday. The accomplishments of its urban base can be seen in the fact that it was an established part of the town centre long before much of the urban regeneration of Manchester and other northern centres (including Oldham) which occurred from the late nineties.

Some of the fiercest criticisms levelled at the College were on educational and cultural grounds. The catchment area included students living in some of the worst urban housing in Britain whilst, only a matter of miles away, some of their peers were living in picturesque rural comfort. Sceptics were unclear how students from such vastly different socio-economic backgrounds would respond to one another. Similarly, given the demographics within the town, a large number of students would have gone through a significant amount of their previous educational lives in establishments which almost exclusively consisted of either white pupils or those of Asian heritage. Again questions were asked about whether students who came from such different and, in some cases, exclusive backgrounds could successfully work together.

Before 1992, sixth form provision in Oldham was decentralized, and many schools were resistant to losing established, in some cases successful, sixth forms. The loss of funding and experienced staff resulted in several outspoken "Save our Sixth Form" campaigns being launched. Despite such initial opposition, Oldham Sixth Form College emerged as one of the most successful and respected institutions within the town and the county. Indeed, during and after the disturbances in Oldham during May 2001 the college was held up as a beacon locally, regionally and nationally, an example of how an institution is capable of encouraging social engagement and defusing potential racial and socio-economic tensions that can exist within culturally mixed and deprived urban areas. This was partly achieved through creating an integrated, tolerant institution based on an atmosphere of academic achievement and tolerance.

Strength in Diversity: Accommodating and Facilitating Multiculturalism within a Secular Setting

Inevitably, given the ethnic and cultural diversity amongst staff and students, a wide variety of religious perspectives are represented. Clarity and transparency became absolute necessities. One of the reasons that OSFC has been able to integrate people from such a wide variety of backgrounds is that all groups come to know that they are respected and will be treated impartially. Coupled with this is the fact that this is unambiguously experienced to be the case; the groups involved clearly feel at ease with a policy based on equality and do their best to apply it in every situation. This is not complicated; it has been talked about (and introduced) with varying degrees of success in a wide variety of political, institutional and social settings. But where it has failed (or has been only partly successful), it may be because its basis in the equal value of every person has never been explicitly agreed, only acted on implicitly, and this has ironically created suspicion rather than relieving tension. Pragmatism clearly has an important role to play in OSFC's attitude towards multiculturalism, but first the principle of *secularism* has to become embedded at grass roots and institutional levels. A relaxed multicultural community can only develop, it was argued, if its members are clear that no religious or sectarian perspective will be promoted or undermined at the expense of any other tradition.

Once the unquestioned fact of secularism has been established, then the religious requirements of any student or interest group can be sympathetically considered and, where appropriate, supported and provided for. This approach has many advantages. First, it can be effectively applied to any religious or cultural setting. Second, provision can be supplied in a unilateral or multilateral fashion depending on the particular situation faced. Examples of this within college life can be seen in the establishment of male and female prayer facilities for Muslim students during Ramadan and the policy that all Muslims students should be entitled to a day's absence in order to celebrate the festival of *Eid ul Fitr* at the end of Ramadan. As a result of ethnic and sectarian differences between different mosques and communities, this festival is commemorated on different days. Through active liaison with the different communities, opportunities were given to all Muslim students with minimum disruption and misunderstanding.

The *Salaam* Society: Calm in the Eye of the Storm?

Oldham Sixth Form College has a vibrant and growing Religious Studies department. In line with national legislation and the requirements of the college's secular ethos, many different religions are represented, with different examination specifications where necessary. An examination of spiritual, atheist and humanist perspectives is also included. The classes are representative of the social and religious make-up of the town and offer good opportunities for fostering positive relations at the expense of prejudicial or discriminatory stereotypes.

Students are given the opportunity to explore Islamic Studies and Philosophy of Religion during the A-Level course and during late 1999 the seeds for the Salaam Society were sown. During an AS class discussion exploring the issues facing Muslims in Britain, a debate developed about depictions of race in the media. More specifically, discussion focused on whether the character of Ali G was to be considered racist or not. Some of the students very articulately expressed the view that it was a satire and should be responded to as such. Others, however, equally forcefully, asserted that Ali G merely perpetuated negative racial stereotypes in the media. Unsurprisingly, despite a very enlightening discussion, the issue was unresolved and we ran out of time to do it justice. The students however, stated that they wanted a place to continue discussing relevant topics of their own choosing that were not prescribed for the examination. They said that there was little or no opportunity to discuss with their peers religious and social issues that personally concerned them, whether in the community, in local *madrassas* (schools or study groups affiliated with mosques), or in the college itself.

In the summer term of 2000 a group of Muslims approached the OSFC management team about setting up an Islamic Society. A Christian Union, involving a member of staff, had already become well established within the college. Given the varying sectarian and ethnic differences within the group, careful consideration was given to this request. The college's explicitly secular outlook meant that a decision was made not to link the group to any particular mosque or ethnic group; also, whilst the group was to be essentially Islamic in character it was also to be explicitly inclusive and open to all regardless of religious background. The Course Leader for Religious Studies (Rob Thorne, an Islamic Studies specialist) was brought in to supervise and guide the group. This was to check that it remained balanced and to ensure that it was not in any way proselytizing within the college. This was considered to be the role of the mosques rather than an OSFC discussion group. It was also crucial to establish that the group was not being used as a mouthpiece for any kind of extremism or radicalization.

One of the most important aspects of the group was to be its name. A title such as the Islamic Society was seen as exclusive, discouraging those having little or no knowledge of Islam from joining and being too reminiscent of a mosque or *madrasa* study group. It was thought that this might lead to misunderstanding about the group's aims whilst also treading on the toes of other similarly named groups connected with some local mosques. It was decided that the title of the group was to be "The *Salaam* Society: The Islamic Issues Enrichment Group". *Salaam* is the Arabic word for peace which is familiar to all Muslim students and demonstrates the explicitly Islamic basis of the group while hinting that it was also open to non-Muslim students. Other subtle aspects of the title were the fact that students were informally exploring Islamic issues rather than actually doing 'Islamic Studies' and therefore not supplanting the more formal examinations offered by both the local madras

as and OSFC itself. Crucially it was decided that the *Salaam* Society was to be an integral part of the OSFC Enrichment Programme. Here, all members of the college community are actively encouraged to engage and interact with one another as part of an officially endorsed college activity. The initial sessions were very well received and included an open debate with the principal, Nick Brown, along with a presentation from well-respected community leaders.

Timetabling commitments meant that Rob Thorne was unable to run the *Salaam* Society until the following September. However it was considered an interesting and exciting opportunity that was well worth pursuing at OSFC. The disturbances in Oldham in May 2001 had meant that students wanted and needed a relaxed, safe place to discuss Islamic, racial, and community issues. The Society was publicized college-wide in September with the first session scheduled for 3pm on Wednesday 12th September 2001.

Finding Our own Voices: Student Representation and Expression of Controversial Topics

The cataclysmic events in New York and Washington on 11th September 2001 represented something of an acid test for OSFC's multicultural policies as well as the strength of relations within the institution. The response of Muslim students was uncertain, as was the potential reaction of their non-Muslim peers. An example of the sensitive and volatile nature of the issues that were prevalent in 2001 was well illustrated by a Muslim student (who was not a member of the *Salaam* Society at the time but went on to study the course in 2003) who confided her fears for the Muslim community to Rob Thorne "This makes me so angry! What has happened is so wrong! We have just got back on our feet after the riots. Now what will people think? We just don't need this!" The situation seemed to be in a serious state of flux.

Despite much serious discussion and a huge amount of soul searching by everyone involved, the sessions following 9/11 were successful. This is indicative of the practical and technical successes of the *Salaam* Society as a whole. A simple way of describing the ethos of the Society is that it is a reflection on a micro level of the multicultural policies that the college demonstrates on the macro level. No one position is to be exclusively expressed at the expense of any other religious, cultural or political perspective. The simple maxim that is initially established within the group is "Just because you say it louder than anybody else doesn't mean that your argument is any more convincing or any truer than anybody else's perspective." Everybody has a right to feel safe; direct or indirect intimidation of any student or statement is prohibited. These maxims of freedom of expression and freedom from intimidation go hand in hand with OSFC's fundamental secular principles.

Pragmatism in dealing with its students is another defining principle of OSFC which is also reflected within the *Salaam* Society. Any perspective can be expressed within the group as long as it can be reasonably justified and the person expressing it is prepared to listen to others and potentially reassess their own position. As a result of this an atmosphere of trust gradually develops within the group. The students themselves decide what issues to explore and what should be tackled at which part of the course. This is crucial in maintaining student participation and attendance.

The group has developed successfully since the initial sessions in 2001 exploring, among other things, Muslim culture in Britain. There was also a session on Islamophobia and Muslims in the media. A particularly important session was when students from a variety of religious backgrounds met and had a small meal (*Kosher* food is also considered to be *Halal*) with a Jewish member of staff, Adrian Soloman. This very personal engagement between people did much to dispel some anti-Semitic stereotypes and had a profound effect upon many of those involved. The group also visited St Patrick's Roman Catholic Church where they explored the similarities between Irish Catholic experiences in Oldham during the 1830s with experiences of Muslims living in Oldham today. A number of visiting speakers have also addressed the group including Fr Philip Sumner. A particular highlight was when the internationally renowned Islamic Studies scholar Professor Hugh Goddard delivered a lecture entitled 'Christian-Muslim relations: Conflict or Co-existence?' The course was very well received with the students particularly enjoying the guest speakers and the opportunity to engage with and explore issues with their peers.

However, one of the major challenges facing a group such as the *Salaam* Society or any other similar group is the issue of representation. Initially, there was some objection to Rob Thorne leading the group. A very small number of students thought that, because he was not Asian or a practising Muslim, it was not appropriate for him to run the group. This was a difficult issue but, as always, was dealt with openly, directly and unambiguously. Several key facts were emphasized. First, the purpose of the group was not to proselytize. Not only was this inappropriate in the context of the college ethos, but it was in fact that the legitimate concern of the local mosques. If students were looking for this sort of material then they could approach a number of organizations that are dedicated to this purpose. It was also emphasized that the group was not an Islamic prayer or study circle but was merely an opportunity to explore Islamic issues in a wider context. With this inmind, the leader's religious and racial identity became irrelevant. OSFC absolutely refuses to prescribe any task on the grounds of race or gender. The argument that Mr Thorne was an inappropriate leader was also completely erroneous in Islamic terms given that the Qur'an is quite explicit that all races are equal in the sight of Allah. Consequently, any exclusionist attitude in the group on the grounds of race is absolutely unacceptable on any level. This controversy was useful in highlighting some of the aims of the group. The group seeks to explore profound areas of similarity and difference between Islam and other world views on a variety of topics. Whilst it can be helpful to find and explore areas of similarity, it can also be productive to deepen the group's understanding of something if areas of profound difference are openly and honestly explored. The session the group held on the Arab–Israeli conflict is a good example of this.

Simply put, the ethos of the group in terms of representation was this: it was not setting out to "represent" any specific interest group. Rob Thorne, who set up the clear aims of the group, was not a practising Muslim and could not 'tell' the group what life for young Muslims was like. Instead he (and ultimately the group as a whole) learnt from each other by clarifying and establishing differing views about the issues involved. This grew as a bond of trust developed throughout the group as members realized that it was a safe environment to raise any question or introduce any topic including (or sometimes especially) those issues which were difficult or emotive. This is something which is strongly reflected in the experiences of students who have been members of the *Salaam* Society and set out at the end of this chapter.

Many Voices: Can You Hear Us?

Given that the *Salaam* Society reinforces and is reinforced by OSFC multicultural policies it has been, and will continue to be, a stable part of the life of the college and is an invaluable grass roots indicator of opinions, attitudes, and tensions within the community. The society mirrors OSFC in that it consists of a number of varied, sometimes disparate voices expressing a myriad of opinions. The 2006 Cantle Report emphasized OSFC's success in getting pupils to relate and engage positively with each other.[2]

The *Salaam* Society also mirrors Oldham Sixth Form College in representing a shared space for an inspiring but potentially volatile mix of races dealing with religious, social, and political issues. Whilst this might be considered by some to be the Society's Achilles heel, it is in fact its greatest strength. Both the *Salaam* Society and OSFC attempt to meet students face to face in their own place and on their own terms. Here the strict imposition of rules and high standards of behaviour are employed to overcome differences and tensions. However, despite the imposition of these expectations of behaviour, individual students, opinions, religions, and cultures are supported and encouraged by a deeply pragmatic and practical approach. In each 15-week session of the *Salaam* Society every separate cohort of the Society has wanted, and in some cases needed, to express itself in different ways. This growing maturity in approaching and tackling sensitive issues through the work of OSFC and other organizations in the town is beginning to have a positive effect. As Tariq Rafique, acting director of the Oldham Race Equality Partnership, says: "Oldham has come a long way since 2001. People accept that we need to interact and integrate more. You can see the positive signs of communities living together. People from all backgrounds are more confident to come forward and report hate crime."[3]

The result of all this has been that the *Salaam* Society, like OSFC itself, has incorporated many different people in numerous ways. The nature of the organization means that the many voices within it never express a single, "one size fits all" message. Given what this egalitarian and democratic Society is trying to achieve such approaches would be completely inappropriate and ultimately impossible. Indeed it is quite legitimate to argue that trying to achieve "one message" in this context would be ultimately self-defeating.

So what do the many voices of the *Salaam* Society express and what if anything can they achieve? Well, it does not and will not express one single message; instead, all its members have consistently expressed similar needs which can be summarized as follows: "We have a voice and want a safe space to be heard. Please listen to what we have to say."

But clearly moving towards developing a constructive community dialogue within an institution involves much more than establishing a discussion group and providing tea and biscuits. It is, however, an achievable process if it is undertaken and exists within a clear and progressive framework. The success of OSFC has demonstrated that it is essential that members of staff have informal points of contact within the establishment. Informal dialogue between different groups is vital in trying to establish if there are any underlying concerns that would make airing certain issues particularly difficult. It can be very useful when such members of staff are involved in the discussion group. If they are not, however, they can be instrumental in assessing responses throughout the community as a whole.

Also, honest and open dialogue between staff and students about the establishment of the group is needed. All parties should endeavour to discover the motivations and outline a clear set of aims and objectives for the group. This is important because while the students involved have an active role and feel "ownership" of the group, it is crucial that the organization itself has active control of the output of the group and can directly influence its behaviour, tone, and content. It is a good idea to establish some sort of constitution, or at the very least set precedents for behaviour that all members of the group are expected to follow. Following this, staff and students can negotiate a variety of topics which they wish to debate or explore. At the initial discussion group, meeting staff and students may choose what to explore from the pre-established topics. Here again the students have "ownership" of the group but, if necessary, can be guided and/or supervised by a member of staff. Engaging both staff and students is recognized as promoting positive values. As well as engaging students within the college itself, it is also vital that the group be given opportunities to interact with those outside: "Community Engagement is intrinsic to community cohesion. Community engagement is a term that refers to a range of processes and activities carried out with, or between people, that make up communities."[4]

Engagement is Crucial

Here can be seen the role that engagement plays in developing community cohesion; a group like the *Salaam* Society can do much to develop this harmony. Indeed, Ofsted recognizes that if an institution "is to successfully fulfil its duty to promote community cohesion, it should focus on . . . faith, ethnicity and culture and socio-economic factors".[5] The personalized nature of a group like the *Salaam* Society also means that these areas can be addressed directly and engagement can take place between both staff and students in approaching these issues, thus helping to develop a positive ethos within the institution. The Cantle Report 2006 recognized that that is particularly strong at OSFC: "Much is to be learned from Oldham Sixth Form College in getting pupils to better relate to each other in school hours."[6]

A welcome benefit of such engagement is the success of the institution that encourages it. The Ritchie Report 2001 asserts that through the success of OSFC and partners an increasing number of young people are continuing to higher education.[7] The importance of young people engaging with one another either formally through established religious education or informally through other initiatives cannot be underestimated therefore. And as the findings of a survey on community relations in Oldham discovered,

> Encouragingly, attitudes are much more positive among young people which bodes well for the future of the Borough. The findings suggest that this is linked to experience of interaction with people from different ethnic backgrounds, which is also much more prevalent among younger people. This suggests that initiatives which promote positive interaction may have an important role to play in further influencing the development of positive attitudes towards diversity and integration.[8]

One of the strengths of a discussion group of this kind is that the students begin to see topics in shades of grey. The result of this reasoning is that students begin to look beyond simply accepting prescriptively a given set of facts or issues. They begin to think issues through on their own terms instead of merely pinning their flags to political, religious, sectarian or ethnic masts merely because they think that is what they think the wider community (whatever that may be) expects of them. This type of educative engagement has been recognized as vital if the community is successfully going to integrate and participate in wider society.[9]

Another valuable benefit of this process is that those involved are given the opportunity to "think outside the box". In the group members can articulate, listen to, and debate issues in a way that might be impossible or inappropriate in other settings. Thus, the group can become a forum for the expression of broader concerns and issues and the students know that their views are taken seriously. The result of this is that the inclusive nature of the institution can be demonstrated, developed, and strengthened.

Phrases such as "I don't want to offend anybody but . . ." along with lengthy pregnant pauses with members of the group reluctant to say anything through the risk of being viewed as racist, controversial, or anti or pro a religious stance are common at the beginning of any discussion group. Particularly today, in a climate of "political correctness", the fear of saying the wrong thing at the wrong time often strangles debate and prevents people from expressing their own deeply held convictions. The issue of perceptions of women in Islam is a good example of a topic that can provoke very strong opinions amongst Muslim and non-Muslim members of the *Salaam* Society alike. Here the role of the leader is crucial; the group must trust that person to be balanced and fair-minded, one who will allow free speech whilst being aware of and sympathetic to the sensibilities to all of those in the group. As has already been illustrated with the debate surrounding Rob Thorne's leadership of the *Salaam* Society, tackling difficult and controversial issues head on builds up trust within the group and demonstrates clearly that different (sometimes difficult) topics will be seriously addressed. Similarly, it shows that within the shared space nobody is to be victimized, intimidated or made to feel uncomfortable. Through acceptance and demonstration of these principles the shared space of the group becomes a safe space which is vital if students are to start to tackle sensitive or difficult issues. If this does not happen students will feel that important issues will just be fudged or side-stepped and their opinions on sensitive topics will simply be fobbed off or disregarded. Virtually any issue can be tackled within a discussion group provided that rigorous standards of appropriate behaviour have been established and are upheld. This must be supplemented with a deep sense of honesty and trust pervading the group. If these conditions are met then any shared space will automatically become a safe space.

Conclusion

The formula outlined here for developing constructive community dialogue need not be applied just to race relations or interfaith debate, although admittedly these are areas in which these concepts are particularly useful. They can, for instance, be equally well applied in a primary school tackling an issue such as bullying. Alternatively, staff may use this process to examine controversial issues such as the management style or structure of a particular organization. Central to the success of engagement of this kind is that it is based on the view that everyone is responsible for their own opinions and that all opinions, within the right context, need to be listened to. Responding to diverse perspectives in this way requires much respect and trust. Valuable discourse can only be achieved if an institution has the intellectual and social courage of its convictions to try and develop understanding by rejecting a simpler pragmatic or piecemeal approach. If and when these rigorous prerequisites are met, it is perfectly possible for many different voices to share the same safe space and engage in constructive community dialogue together. I end with students' stimulating and heartening accounts about their membership of the *Salaam* Society:

- *Salaam* – a famous greeting amongst Muslims all around the world was the base of our weekly events. Literally meaning "peace", it was the foundation of our classes.

- What intrigued me about this particular enrichment group was the fact that it was different and something I had never come across before. I felt this was the opportunity to express my beliefs and feelings in a safe and open environment. It was comforting to know that others shared my same feelings, even in times of contrast; the people were always eager to hear my views, as much as I was eager to hear theirs. The open minded people were very welcoming to different beliefs. I enjoyed listening to the different views put forward by the diverse range of students.
- Some of the world issues we discussed consisted of the rise of Obama, the fall of the twin towers and the ever lasting beauty of Islamic art and architecture. Our gatherings were not just restricted to the class room as we took it to a much wider place of learning: the world itself. We watched a range of documentaries in order to gain insights of events that shook the world, to broaden our understanding of the real world and to inspire us to become our better selves. We also watched a play that manifested all we had discussed; it was enjoyable and very inspiring to see our thoughts come to life.
- In a nutshell; it was an informal discussion group that explored Islamic and other religious issues in the media in order to deepen our understanding of the world around us. It provided us with a way to reflect on and ponder over things that we would never have really thought about, but affect us none the less.
- The *Salaam* Society was both interesting and entertaining through debate and discussions on documentaries regarding different current affairs affecting Islam. It was enlightening to see others opinions and have a chance to voice my own. The main thing that stood out for me was the discussions – they were *engaging* and useful.

I would like to acknowledge the following who have assisted towards the writing of this chapter and to the continued success of the Salaam Society: Danielle Sullivan; my family; OSFC; Oldham Interfaith Forum; Jade Cross; Khushnooda Zaman; Rachel Briggs; Dr James Crossley; Canon R.F. Thorne; Prof. Hugh Goddard; Rev. Derrick Peel; Shamim Miah; and Adrian Solomon. I would also like to dedicate this chapter to Nick Brown, OBE, in profound gratitude for his faith in me and constant support he has always shown. I have been just one of the many Oldhamers who have benefited from the innumerable opportunities he has provided through his work in the town.

Notes

1 *The Independent on Sunday* 1026 (25th October 2009): 8.
2 www.oldham.gov.uk/cantle-review-final-report.pdf: 9. Accessed 23 October 2009.
3 *The Independent on Sunday* 1026 (25th October 2009): 9.
4 Oldham Community Cohesion Advisory Group Annual Report 07/08 – www.oldhampartnership.org.uk/oldham_ccag_annual_report_07-08.pdf: 3. Accessed 24 October 2009.
5 *Inspecting Maintained Schools' Duty to Promote Community Cohesion: Guidance for Inspectors* – http://www.ofsted.gov.uk/content/download/6795/70129/file/cokmmunityCohesiion_Guidance_Feb09.doc: 4. Accessed 25 October 2009.
6 The Cantle Report – www.oldham.gov.uk/cantle-review-final-report.pdf: 9. Accessed 25 October 2009.
7 The Ritchie Report – http://www.oldhamir.org.uk/OIR%20Repport.pdf: 34. Accessed 26 October 2009.
8 Community Relations in Oldham 2005. Oldham Metropolitan Borough. Findings from your "You and Your Community Survey" – http://www.oldham.gov.uk/key_findings_on_community_cohesion.pdf: 1. Accessed 26 October 2009.
9 R. Briggs. 2007. 'Why are we so scared of the Respect Party? Why dissent is our best hope for a cohesive Britain', *Renewal* 15(2/3): 95.

Chapter Four

Getting to Know You . . .

Joy Schmack

In the Rodgers and Hammerstein musical *The King and I* Anna has been brought from England to Siam where she is to teach the King's children. The culture is new to her and she arrives with many misconceptions and hesitancies. The song 'Getting to Know You' is sung by Anna as she recognizes that it is through meaningful engagement with the princes and princesses that new insights will be gained and preconceptions challenged. This chapter explores the opportunities that visits to synagogues can generate in not only engaging with faith members but also in challenging misconceptions and stereotypes. It argues that fundamental to this process are clearly devised objectives relevant to pupils' needs in their evolving attempts to make sense of their own world. The chapter continues by exploring the role of the "faith host" and, in particular, the nature of their encounter with visiting pupils. The importance of opportunities to create "shared worlds" is highlighted as a key component of community cohesion.

Throughout the chapter there are constant references to the highly developed skills necessitated in the organization and implementation of effective visits. The crucial role of teacher as visionary, orchestrater, engager, and challenger can sometimes be overshadowed by their role as a completer of countless forms and risk assessments.

At the time of writing the Department of Children, Schools and Families (DCSF) are fervently endorsing the importance of learning outside the classroom for pupils of all key stages within English schools. Conferences are being organized, leaflets sent into schools and websites set up to encourage teachers to organize visits to support all areas of the curriculum. The Learning Outside the Classroom Manifesto (2006) (lotc.org.uk) consists of ten strands reflecting areas of the curriculum. As the name would imply it is the Sacred Space strand which particularly focusses upon the relationship between visiting places of worship and religious education. Guidance that has been published to support the implementation of the Manifesto identifies two specific benefits of school visits. Not only do they support effective learning in religious education but they also aid community cohesion by giving opportunities for interaction with faith communities.

> Visiting sacred spaces is primarily associated with learning in religious education where young people engage with living religions and meet members of faith communities to learn about their beliefs, rituals of worship and celebrations.[1]

Similar endorsements to teachers can be found in the influential National Framework for Religious Education (QCA, 2004). Although these guidelines are non-statutory they have a direct influence on locally agreed syllabi and the new GCSE specifications. The recommendations and learning opportunities described in each of the four Key Stages make reference to the positive role that visits to places of worship play in effective and engaging Religious Education. For example:

> All courses should provide opportunities within and beyond school for learning that involves first hand experiences and activities involving people, places and events (for example the local area, places of worship and community activities). (QCA, 2004: 31)

Such advocacy is hardly a new phenomenon. Indeed, for the previous two decades it has been one of the few consistent messages in the ever changing world of religious education in England.

The benefits of visiting places of worship have been relayed to teachers through:

- Pedagogical guidance for teachers

> Whatever visit you finally plan, it will greatly enrich and enhance your teaching about Judaism. (Jackson and Starkings, 1990: 121)

- The compilation of directories of local places of worship by SACREs and distributed to schools, such as those compiled for places of worship in Croydon (2000) and Liverpool (2009)
- Locally agreed syllabus recommendations, as in the Gloucestershire agreed syllabus for RE (2006), which identifies meeting visitors and going on visits to faith communities as a key learning experience and one of the essential experiences and opportunities for all pupils; and last, but certainly not least, through
- Ofsted inspection reports on schools

> They gain a practical understanding of cultural and religious diversity by visiting places of worship. (Ofsted, 2008)

Uniquely, for religious education there appears to be a united voice from the DCSF, the QCA, Ofsted, and local SACREs – a voice that is stating clearly and consistently that visits to places of worship play an important role in effective religious education. But what are the purposes of such visits? Despite the aforementioned united endorsement there is a paucity of research to answer this question and to assess long and short term impact. Indeed, do there need to be specific purposes? Or is it, as one of the teachers interviewed stated, just a reward for good behaviour?

> There isn't a particular purpose to the visit. It's like the treat at the end of the unit of work. Those pupils who don't behave during RE lessons in that term don't go.[2]

One of the most commonly stated benefits for school pupils visiting synagogues rests upon the importance of meeting faith members. Gateshill and Thompson (2000: 5), for example, refer to the significant contribution that can be made to cultural awareness and community cohesion:

> Meeting people from different cultures can be an enlightening experience for pupils. It may be the first time they have met someone from a culture different from their own.

This role is replicated in the recommendations of the National Framework:

> The presence of members of different faiths should be welcomed as an asset in religious education, and in the dialogue between faiths local resources inside and outside the school should be used to the full. (QCA, 2004: 63)

Whilst similarly confirming the importance of meeting faith members, teacher trainees indicated two distinct purposes of the encounter:

- In order to learn more about the faith (Judaism) as the host is perceived as an expert.
- In order to meet a member(s) of the faith tradition to break down stereotypes, prejudices and aid community cohesion.

Each of these objectives will now be further considered.

"Getting to know you, getting to know all about you"

There was unanimous agreement from the teacher trainee responses that it was important for a member of the faith community to show the class around the synagogue thereby acting as a "faith host". Responses often made reference to how the "faith host" would possess the knowledge to answer pupils' questions. Indeed several respondents referred to the "faith host(s)" as "experts in Judaism".

It is, perhaps naturally, often assumed that a faith member will have an informed knowledge and understanding of their faith tradition. The importance of the insider voice in highlighting the distinctive nuances of a religious tradition has long been established. This can be particularly significant in the teaching of Judaism because textbooks which are used in schools are often written by Gentiles and can be prone to misconceptions and distortions. Fisher (1993) illustrates an inclination to "Christianize" Jewish festivals and present distortions of religious practices. Indeed, only recently the *Jewish Chronicle* reported that a textbook used by 5,000 students in Australia stated that polygamy was prevalent in Israel and that during Passover Jews kill lambs and spread the blood on doorposts (Goldberg, 2009). The importance of reflecting the insider perspective is identified in the introduction to the seminal *Model Syllabuses for Religious Educatiuon*. The distinct contribution that a Jewish faith group can make to the accurate representation of its tradition is clearly argued:

> each faith group has chosen the areas of study it considers essential to gain an understanding of its religious traditions. Previously choices were often made by educationalists and publishers in an ad hoc way. For example, Hanukkah is not a major festival within Judaism, and yet is treated as such within many classrooms. (SCAA, 1994: 3)

Although an insider voice has the potential to present an authentic perspective of the faith tradition there is no guarantee that a sufficiently broad or accurate picture is represented. As Schneider (2005) cautions when considering strategies to challenge stereotyping:

> Am I likely to find out more about Native Americans by meeting a few and discussing their lives, or by watching a good documentary that presents a wider range of people and experiences than I could encounter on my own? The answer is not obvious.

Critical awareness is needed by teachers to identify the personal convictions and religious interpretations of the "faith host" and to be able to place these within a broader context for pupils. Usually the "faith hosts" are volunteers who do not set themselves up as experts. Many would be unable to give the type of explanations which are often demanded by locally agreed syllabi or Examination Boards. An illustration of this was given by a Head of Religious Education in a large school in the north-west of England:

> We planned to take the year 11's to the synagogue to act as a revision aid before they sat their GCSE examination in Judaism. One of our pupils, obviously keen to understand the application of kashrut, asked the guide "What did you have for breakfast?" The response was "bacon butties". There was an audible cry of dismay from the teachers. Yes, the answer indicated the practice of our host but it wasn't going to be marked as correct in the GCSE exam.

"Faith hosts", it must be remembered, speak on behalf of themselves, about their own experiences and their own faith journey. This process can result in the presentation of personalized and sometimes idiosyncratic versions of religions to pupils and has been criticized by Grimmitt (2000) when discussing the strong involvement of faith representatives in the production of the model syllabuses in England and Wales. Although not always apparent from resources used in the classroom it must be remembered that Judaism is a diverse tradition with many different practices and cultural influences. It would be unfeasible for a "faith host" to do justice to the full spectrum of beliefs, values and traditions. As Jackson contends:

> Clearly we need to go to accounts of religious faith and tradition from insiders. But even here the sources need to be set in a wider context, since what individual can speak on behalf of a whole religious tradition? Insiders may represent a unique perspective, but their accounts may also reflect the views of particular institutions, denominations, sects or movements. Insider accounts may also have particular ethnic characteristics and cultural emphases. (2004: 134)

Indeed, previous experiences would suggest that some "faith hosts" consciously decline to refer to a range of Jewish traditions in order that the practices and traditions of their own sub-group appear the "true" or "authentic" Judaism. Jackson expresses concern that those within the tradition might sometimes have a rigid view in presenting the tradition through their own limited or stereotyped experiences and can be particularly representative of the ethnic group that they belong to.

> The difficulty for individuals to speak and negotiate authentically on behalf of those who identify themselves with a particular religion is clear. Individuals could act in the interests of a particular sub-group, perhaps to promote a particular ideological viewpoint, or in their own interests.(Jackson, 2004: 134)

Presenting any religious tradition as homogenous is detrimental to community cohesion. Making a group appear uniform creates an exaggeration of the differences between the insider group (such as Jews) and outsider group (such as the pupils). Wood (2007: 3) suggests that this reinforces a "threat element" as the group being learnt about appears "a single monolithic bloc, static and unresponsive to new realities".

By implication therefore the members of the Jewish faith might appear a united force and such a representation can produce a fertile breeding ground for misconceptions and stereotypes which can lead to prejudice and antisemitism. How ironic it is therefore that a further commonly cited purpose of meeting faith members is to break down stereotypes, prejudices and aid community cohesion. As we shall see, the formation of misconceptions is a complex process. A one-off encounter with members of faith traditions could have little positive effect and, indeed, can serve to reinforce existing misconceptions. The process of organizing visits therefore requires careful planning considerations which represent the distinct needs of the pupils.

"Getting to like you, hoping that you'll like me"

For over 50 years social psychologists (e.g. Allport, 1954) have argued that some forms of contact in some places will reduce prejudices. The importance of face to face meetings to break down stereotypes was recognized by Lippmann (1922) and has been frequently advanced as a means of enhancing positive relationships and tackling prejudice (Allport, 1954; Towles-Schwen and Fazio, 2001).

Similarly, guidance documents in religious education frequently endorse the positive impact meeting faith members can have on anti-racist education and community cohesion. The seminal Schools Council Working Paper 36 argued that pupils should "meet people from other faiths in a bid to dismantle 'European tribalism'" (Schools Council, 1971).

Teachers' handbooks have frequently affirmed this view, contending that previously held misconceptions and prejudices which can lead to antisemitism will be eradicated. Gateshill and Thompson (2000: 5) state that "in our experience through visits to places of worship, bridges can be built and prejudices and stereotypes cast aside".

It could be argued that there has never been a more appropriate time in the United Kingdom for prejudices and stereotypes of Jews to be "cast aside".

Antisemitism is not a new phenomena. Beller (2007: 1) states that "it has stretched across millennia and across continents". But it is certainly not a phenomenon found only in the past. The aptly titled Runnymede report *A Very Light Sleeper* (1994) illustrated the persistence and dangers of antisemitism. Alarmingly, a decade later the All-Party Parliamentary Inquiry into Antisemitism commenced their *Report* (2006) by stating that

> Until recently the prevailing opinion both within the Jewish community and beyond was that anti-Semitism had receded to the point that it existed only on the margins of society. However, the evidence we received indicates that there has been a reversal of the progress since the year 2000, which has created anxiety and concern within the Jewish community.

Three years later the Jewish Community Security Trust recorded a "record rise in anti-semitism" with attacks in the United Kingdom doubling in the first half of the year compared with the same period in 2008.[3]

Recognition of this prevailing situation must be at the forefront of every teacher's mind when planning visits to synagogues. It is imperative that learning and teaching strategies are planned (rather than left to chance) to challenge pupil misconceptions which can so often lead to prejudices and antisemitism.

Lack of personal contact with Jews can exacerbate antisemitism. Despite the readmittance of Jews to England over 350 years ago there remains a very small presence. In consequence, many pupils (and teachers) have knowingly had little or no personal contact with Jews. Such limited contact experience was reflected in the responses from the PGCE teacher trainees. Only 44% (49 responses) believed they had ever personally met a Jew although, it needs to be remembered, they were teaching about Judaism in their placement schools. The representation of Jews through the media exacerbates the dangers of such limited contact. Television is a powerful tool for people in making sense of their world (Bandura, 1994). The Mori Report (2005) claimed that for 80% of young people in England and Wales television was their main source of knowledge of the world. So who are the Jews represented in the media that might be informing pupils' conceptions and misconceptions? The PGCE teacher trainees were asked to identify five Jews whom they were aware of. Those most frequently referred to were

Adam Sandler, Ben Stiller, Ross from *Friends*, Monica from *Friends*, Sasha Baron Cohen, Alan Sugar, David Baddiel, Woody Allen, Krusty the clown (from *The Simpsons*), Simon Amstell, and Uri Geller. A brief analysis of the responses would note

- The only female referred to was the fictional character of Monica from the American comedy series *Friends*.
- A number of examples are American.
- All of the Jews indicated are connected with show business (mainly comedy).

Such a narrow perspective could lead to the formation of structured stereotypes which do not represent a variety of faith members. If the teacher trainees have no other points of reference then they are going to be unable to broaden the perspectives of their pupils.

If, as previously stated, the main object of the visit to the synagogue is for pupils to encounter members of the faith community, then it is vital that the contact is meaningful. Government guidance on promoting community cohesion identifies the importance of inter-group contact using a sliding scale of levels of effective engagement:

- for conversations to go beyond surface friendliness
- for people to exchange personal information or talk about each other's differences and identities
- where people share a common goal or an interest
- where contacts are sustained over a long term (one-off chance meetings are unlikely to make a difference) (DCSF, 2007)

It is this final point that is particularly significant when considering frequent classroom practice.

"Getting to know you, Getting to feel free and easy"

The reported increase in antisemitism in Britain includes a rise in attacks on synagogues. In 2007 the Jewish Community Trust reported that 33 synagogues were desecrated during the year – a rise of 24 on the previous year. A direct consequence has been more vigilant security on all synagogues and Jewish activities. It has therefore become even more difficult for visitors to enter a synagogue without prior arrangement and security checks. In previous years it has been noticeable how many teacher trainees have little or no personal experience of visiting a synagogue despite the praiseworthy intentions of Jewish Heritage Week. Of the 131 PGCE teacher trainees interviewed, 82% (96) had never visited a synagogue and 98% (113) had never attended an act of worship in a synagogue. The high number is of particular concern as the respondents were all teaching RE. We have already noted how lack of contact can perpetuate misconceptions. How many pupils must wonder what activities and practices happen behind the, often closed, doors of synagogues? As Isadora Duncan remarked, "What one has not experienced, one will never understand in print."

The lack of personal experience can become fertile territory for generating misconceptions which are prone to being exacerbated by antisemitic media. One website, accessible to pupils, refers to Jews as "Satan Worshippers", lists the addresses of all the synagogues in the United Kingdom, and states that "Synagogues are one of the many fronts used by the global Jewish shadow government to conduct their criminal and subversive activities against whichever host nation they happen to reside with."[4]

For pupils visiting a synagogue as part of their religious education programme this can have immense implications. It could be a once in a lifetime occurrence, a singular opportunity to see behind the doors and witness the diverse ways the community supports and engages in local, national, and global activities. Once behind the doors the way is open to a range of learning opportunities not only for religious education but for social, moral and spiritual development. Too often, however, the structure of the visit comprises a "Cook's Tour" around the synagogue with, if coach parking allows, the chance for a few questions. Arguably a unique opportunity is missed. The correlation between engagement of pupils and effective learning is well documented but often pupils adopt the role of passive learners and listeners. Let us look at some strategies that could be adopted to develop greater engagement and result in a more effective visit.

Fundamentally, if the objective of the visit is to challenge pupils' misconceptions and stereotypes regarding Jews and Judaism, then surely the teacher must establish what those preconceptions are? Schneider (2005: 209) reflects the rudimentary importance of this diagnostic assessment: "Saying we want to change a stereotype is like saying you want to fix a car but you don't know what the matter of it is."

The nature of prejudices and misconceptions are complex and cannot be generalized from school to school or even class to class. Stephan (1999) argues that stereotype formation comes from a wide range of situations and is informed by many factors such as parents, peer views, and the media. All of this can be exacerbated by limited personal contact experiences. Fisher illustrates the personalised and idiosyncratic nature of stereotypes. He refers to the diagnostic attitudinal testing of Catholic High School pupils in New York. Their responses shared a perception of Jews as "very strict", "mean" and "bossy". The teacher sought to identify how these stereotypes had become prevalent throughout the class.

> After much prodding , it turned out that the youngsters had personally known only one Jew in their lives: their sixth grade teacher! Their negative reactions were not typical of a sixth grader's reaction to Jews as Jews but a reaction to teachers as adult authority figures. (Fisher, 1993: 89)

From the semi-structured interviews conducted with the PGCE trainees it emerged that the most common stereotypes held by their pupils about Jews were "old-fashioned", "greedy", "rich", "male", "exclusive", "self-supportive", "strange", "isolated", and "different", thus reflecting a persistent negative stereotypical schema of Jews (cf. Beller, 2007). The awareness of these distinctive perceptions permits teachers' informed planning to incorporate activities, resources, and learning opportunities which will act as relevant challenge. It is only through diagnostic assessment that a teacher can ensure the contact visit doesn't reaffirm the stereotypes held by learners.[5]

"When I am with you, Getting to know what to say"

Effective community cohesion evolves from groups recognizing their shared worlds, shared experiences, and shared values (Stephan, 1999). Indeed, Zanna (1994) suggested that elements of threat can emerge when specific areas or values appear unshared between the groups. Dialogue enables an understanding of the perspective of others and the recognition of common areas (see Batson and others, 2002; Batson and others, 1997; Galinsky and Moskowitz, 2000). As people start to discuss their backgrounds and points of similarity so they start to build up a relationship and trust. This process can be capitalized on through visits to places of worship by allowing pupils to have a more participatory role rather than, as is so often the case, the teacher acting as intermediary through which dialogue occurs.

Effective interfaith activities have shown the importance of not merely meeting members of different faiths but engaging together on a project which gives a common sense of purpose (see Stephan, 1999). Let us look at some small scale strategies which could be deployed.

It is of elementary importance that before any visit takes place teachers establish meaningful contact with the "faith host". Organizational details can be established but, more importantly, dialogue should confirm the purpose of the visit not only for the teacher but for the "faith host". Through the dialogue a rapport can be established between teacher and "faith host" which will become evident to pupils on their visit and form a model of how they should react. Responses from the teacher trainees often reflected a lack of confidence concerning how they would facilitate a visit to the synagogue and their own encounter with the faith member. Such hesitancy could easily be picked up upon by pupils during the visit. One of the trainees stated:

> It would be really important to take my year 7's to the synagogue but I would want the speaker to take over as soon as we got there. I would be embarrassed in case I am asked a question and I don't know the answer.

Prior meeting(s) with the "faith host" will give opportunities to identify shared experiences between the stake holders. These may be as rudimentary as direct references to shopping patterns, interests in sport, or knowledge of films and music. Classroom displays could then be established with photographs of the "faith hosts", personalized with their name and a brief biography emphasizing the similarities between the world of "faith host" and pupils. For GCSE classes it would be beneficial to include a diverse range of faith members' views on examination issues such as relationships, animal rights, and capital punishment. In this way pupils will be entering a synagogue and meeting with a Jew (possibly for the first time) but will feel they have a point of reference and contact which indeed could remain with them throughout their study of Judaism. Classroom displays depicting the many activities of the synagogues such as charity events and sporting fixtures would raise pupils awareness of shared experiences and shared worlds. Through such preparation pupils would be undertaking the visit in an informed way with an awareness of similarities to their own life experiences.

Learning activities could be incorporated which make dialogue with the "faith host" essential and purposeful. Pupils could be involved in problem solving activities investigating hypothetical questions such as –

- What would be missed if the synagogue closed?
- The community needs a new Rabbi. How should they advertise and interview?
- The synagogue has been given a donation of £5,000. How should it be spent?

In lessons prior to the visit pupils could ascertain what evidence they need to collect and the questions they need to ask the "faith host" in order to produce reasoned answers. Pupils' own contact with the "faith host" would therefore play a pivotal role in the learning experience. As Schneider (2005) suggests, working with others in cooperative groups leads to more positive attitudes and is more likely to constitute exchanges of personalized information, which again reduces threat.

The importance of "pupil voice" is well documented and is now a key source of evidence for any Ofsted inspections. Pupils engage more readily with learning experiences if they have some ownership of purpose, content, and process. There is a significant increase in pupil engagement in religious education if they experience direct involvement with the planning and organization of the topic (see O'Grady, 2003). For pupils to be engaged with the visit, therefore, it is important they feel they have a steering role rather than it being "done" to them. Central to this process would be opportunities for pupils to formulate the objectives for the visit and to ascertain what they want from the experience. Leganger-Krogstad(2003) and Skeie (2002) show that when pupils are allowed to raise their own individual concerns and questions it enables them to make connections to their own "life-world" at their own level. All too often, however, any pupil question time is scheduled for the end of the visit and can appear perfunctory or a time-filler. There can be little interaction with the "faith host" as the teacher often acts as the intermediary throughout the experience. Indeed, some pupils are reluctant to ask the questions that puzzle them as they are concerned that certain questions appear rude. Such reserve can be reinforced by teacher warnings of dire consequences of inappropriate behaviour. This reticence and concern regarding appropriateness was evidenced by the teacher trainees. After a visit to a local synagogue they were asked if there was a question they wanted to ask the "'faith host" but felt might be deemed inappropriate. Over one third of the respondents had a question they had wanted to ask but didn't for fear it was inappropriate. The areas they wanted to ask questions on would all have aided their understanding of Judaism and Jewish life. They can be divided into ten broad categories:

- beliefs (5 responses)
- Zionism (5 responses)
- antisemitism (6 responses)
- the Holocaust (13 responses)
- wearing of kippot (3 responses)
- dietary requirements (3 responses)
- circumcision (3 responses)
- attitudes to other faiths (2 responses)
- views on moral issues (2 responses)
- attitudes to money (2 responses)

Many of the unasked questions reflected misconceptions and stereotypes such as

- Why do you treat Palestinians as you do?
- Do you only wear hats when praying?
- Are all Jews rich? Why?
- Why are so many Jews in show business?
- Why are women treated as second-class citizens?
- How do I as a teacher, or how do you as a member of the Jewish faith, counteract claims that Jewish people are motivated by money and greed?

Regretfully, one wonders if there will ever be another opportunity for these misconceptions to be raised and countered.

Significantly, a further factor prohibiting engagement with the "faith host" was the teacher trainees' uncertainty concerning the appropriate language to be used. Many responses expressed concern that the terms they used wouldn't cause offence. The one most mentioned was if it was appropriate to use the term "Jew". What a pity that issue hadn't been discussed with the "faith host" during the visit! Language is a source of power and controversy (see Wood, 2007). When dealing with issues of racism and antisemitism there is often a preferred choice of words which many pupils (never mind teachers!) may feel they are unsure of. Consequently it is often deemed preferable to say nothing rather than enter into dialogue with faith members and offend.

The potential range of benefits of visits to synagogues has been raised throughout the chapter. Yet, equally palpable is that the gains are not just in terms of religious education but of whole-child personal, moral, social, and spiritual development and of course community cohesion. As such a visit to a synagogue does not necessarily need to be solely the province of the RE department. The implications and outcomes are bigger than that. They are for the whole school, the whole child. As reflected by the grading criteria in the Ofsted Framework for Community Cohesion, the active support of senior management is essential when dealing with any issues concerning commmunty cohesion. The headteacher case study on the sacred space site exemplifies the role that leaders in a school can make with all staff and parents/carers to support the effectiveness of visits.[6] It is possible(even probable) that few members of the teaching staff will have visited a synagogue or engaged with members of the Jewish community. To develop community cohesion visits to synagogues could be organized outside school hours and be open to members of the wider school community including teaching staff, governors, support staff, and parents and carers. Indeed, long-term links could be established through shared ventures between both communities.

Conclusion

Visits to synagogues can be unique opportunities to engage pupils in learning and social development. They are not, as one teacher put it, 'the cherry on top of the icing on top of the cake', nor should they be a reward for good behaviour. They have the potential to develop pupils' understanding of Judaism and, perhaps more importantly, to challenge misconceptions and stereotypes which, if left unchallenged, can lead to prejudices and antisemitism. The key to realizing this potential is to establish opportunities for pupil engagement through activities, curriculum design and meaningful encounters with "faith hosts". The role of the teacher is crucial and the developed skills that are needed are many. This may be a singular opportunity for pupils to visit a synagogue and engage with faith members. It is essential that opportunities are given for pupils to explore those areas that will challenge preconceptions and have the freedom to ask those questions that will help make informed decisions as they make sense of their world.

Notes

1 http://www.lotc.org.uk/Out-and-about-guidance/How-do-we-organise-learning/Framework-for-planning-LOtC-experiences/Where-and-when/Sacred-spaces. Accessed 23 February 2010.
2 Evidence is drawn from semi-structured interviews with practising teachers and responses to questionnaires from primary and secondary Post Graduate Certificate of Education teacher trainees.
3 www.bbc.co.uk/go/pr/fr/-1/hi/uk/8166173.stm. Accessed 23 July 2009.
4 The author has considered it inappropriate to give a direct reference to the website.
5 There are many examples of attitudinal diagnostic assessment that are appropriate for classroom use. Most commonly used are word association, individual questionnaires, and the use of vignettes.
6 The importance of Senior Management's proactive support of visits can be seen in one of the Learning Outside the Classroom case studies at www.lotc.org. As a response to parental resistance to pupils visiting the local mosque the headteacher with the RE co-ordinator organized a plan of action. They arranged for a sequence of visits beginning with whole school staff, then parents and governors, and finally the visit for pupils. The headteacher accompanied all visits. In this way parents and carers could see (probably for the first time) inside a mosque and be able to meet with faith members and ask questions to air any concerns. If parents and carers continued to wish to withdraw their children from the visit they were, at least, making an informed choice rather than basing their actions on preconceptions.

References

Allport, G.W. 1954. *The Nature of Prejudice.* Garden City, NY. Doubleday/Anchor.

Bandura, A. 1994. 'Social Cognitive Theory of Mass Communication', in Bryant, J., and Zillmann, D. (eds). *Media Effects: Advances in Theory and Research.* Hillsdale, NJ. Erlbaum. 61–90.

Batson, C.D., and others. 1997. 'Empathy and Attitudes: Can Feeling for a Member of a Stigmatized Group Improve Feelings toward the Group?', *Journal of Psychology and Social Psychology*, 72: 105–118.

Batson, C.D., and others. 2002. 'Empathy, Attitudes and Action: Can Feeling for a Member of a Stigmatized Group Motivate One to Help the Group?', *Personality and Social Psychology Bulletin,* 72: 105–118.

Beller, S. 2007. *Antisemitism: A Very Short Introduction.* Oxford. Oxford University Press.

Davies, L. 2008. *Educating Against Extremism.* Stoke-on-Trent. Trentham Books.

Davies, L. 2004. *Education and Conflict: Complexity and Chaos.* London. Routledge.

DCSF. 2007. *Guidance on the duty to promote community cohesion.* London. Department for Children, Schools and Families.

Fisher, E. 1993. *Faith Without Prejudice.* New York. Crossroad.

Galinsky, A.D., and Moskowitz, G.B. 2000. 'Perspective-taking: Decreasing Stereotype Expression, Stereotype Accessibility, and In-group Favouritism', *Journal of Personality and Social Psychology*, 78: 706–724.

Gateshill, P., and Thompson, J. 2000. *Visiting Places of Worship.* London. Hodder and Stoughton Educational.

Goldberg, D. 2009. 'Australia textbook "offensive"', *Jewish Chronicle* (29 October). Available on-line at http://www.thejc.com/news/world-news/21428/australia-textbook-offensive'. Accessed 22 February 2010.

Grimmitt, M.H. 2000. 'The Captivity and Liberation of Religious Education and the Meaning of Pedagogy', in Grimmitt, M.H. (ed.). *Pedagogies of Religious Education:Case Studies in the Research and Development of Good Pedagogic Practice in RE.* Great Wakering: McCrimmons.

Jackson, R., and Starkings, D. 1990. *The Junior RE Handbook.* Cheltenham. Stanley Thornes.

Jackson, R. 2004. *Rethinking Religious Education and Plurality.* London. RoutledgeFalmer.

Leganger-Krogstad, H. 2003. 'Dialogue among Young Citizens in a Pluralistic Religious Education Classroom', in Jackson, R. (ed). *International Perspectives on Citizenship Education and Religious Diversity.* London. RoutledgeFalmer.

Linville, P.W. 1982. 'The Complexity-Extremity Effect and Age-Based Stereotyping', *Journal of Personality and Social Psychology*, 42: 192–211.

Lippmann, W. 1922. *Public Opinion.* New York. Harcourt, Brace.

O'Grady, K. 2003. 'Motivation in Religious Education: A Collaborative Investigation with Year Eight Students', *British Journal of Religious Education*, 25(3): 214–225.

Ofsted. 2008. *Kassim Darwish Grammar School for Boys Independent School: Inspection Report.* London. Ofsted.

QCA. 2004. *Religious Education: the Non-Statutory National Framework.* London:

Qualifications and Curriculum Authority.
Report of the All-Party Parliamentary Inquiry into Antisemitism. 2006. London. Stationery Office.
Runnymede Trust. 1994. *A Very Light Sleeper: The Persistence and Dangers of Antisemitism.* London. Runnymede Trust.
SCAA. 1994. *Model Syllabuses for Religious Education: Faith Communities' Working Group Reports.* London. School Curriculum and Assessment Authority.
Schneider, D.J. 2005. *Psychology of Stereotyping.* New York. Guildford Press.
Schools Council. 1971. *Religious Education in Secondary Schools.* Working Paper 36. London. Evans Bros. Methuen Educational.
Skeie, G. 2002. 'The Concept of Plurality and its Meaning for Religious Education', *British Journal of Religious Education*, 25(2): 47–59.
Stephan, W. 1999. *Reducing Prejudice and Stereotyping in Schools.* London. Teachers College Press.
Towles-Schwen, T., and Fazio, R.H. 2001. 'On the Origins of Racial Attitudes: Correlates of Childhood Experiences', *Personality and Social Psychology Bulletin,* 27: 226–241.
Wood, A. 2007. *What Do We Tell The Children? Confusion, Conflict and Complexity.* Stoke-on-Trent. Trentham Books.
Zanna, M. 1994. 'On the Nature of Prejudice', *Canadian Psychology*, 35: 11–23.

Chapter Five

New Religious Movements in the RE Classroom

James D. Holt

This chapter investigates the place of New Religious Movements (NRMs) in the secondary RE classroom (with specific reference to The Church of Jesus Christ of Latter-day Saints and Jehovah's Witnesses[1]). This is an area in which there has been minimal research and publication. The chapter begins by arguing what is meant by the term "New Religious Movement". While acknowledging that the conclusions reached are a matter of some debate, the study seeks to use "NRM" in a non-judgemental and non-pejorative way. The chapter then goes on to discuss the arguments for and against the inclusion of New Religious Movements in the RE classroom. These arguments are based on interviews and questionnaires as part of a research study. Each is given thoughtful consideration and responded to as applicable. The conclusion of this work is that NRMs do have a place in the teaching of RE and suggests a way forward for the inclusion of New Religious Movements in secondary RE.

What is a New Religious Movement?

In beginning any work on NRMs it is important to understand what the term means. Many authors have sought to answer this question (see for example Barker, 2001;[2] Chryssides, 1994[3]). Indeed, it would seem that there are as many definitions as there are authors. For the purposes of this chapter I adopt two criteria which incorporate elements of both Barker and Chryssides' definitions, but also strive to include those traditionally associated within the umbrella term.[4]

1 A NRM has been founded within the past 200 years.
2 A NRM places itself, or is placed by the majority of members of its "parent" faith, outside of the mainstream. (This could be because of tradition and/or doctrine.)

The Debate about NRMs and the RE Classroom

The current situation

Currently there seems to be a distinct lack of mention of NRMs in agreed syllabuses. However, there have been recent additions in a number of agreed syllabuses, for example Nottinghamshire:

> Schools are at liberty to plan to teach using material from more than the minimum number of religions, while having regard to the importance of enabling pupils to study religions in depth.
>
> Schools are advised to select which religions to study in consultation across the primary and secondary phases of education, to enable pupils across the 5–14 age range to learn about each of the six principal religions represented in the United Kingdom (Christianity, Islam, Hinduism, Sikhism, Judaism, Buddhism).
>
> The make up of the local area and the school community is an important influence in planning which religions are selected for study by the school.
>
> Additionally, schools are also at liberty to use material from other religious traditions and belief systems represented in the UK, such as the Baha'i Faith, the Jehovah's Witnesses, or Humanism. (Nottinghamshire County Council, 2003: 19)

While agreed syllabuses may be beginning to recognize the place of NRMs in the family of faiths, not all of the content suggested by an agreed syllabus needs to be covered in a Key Stage and so the inclusion of a NRM into the RE classroom is left to the discretion of the teacher as highlighted above by the phrase "at liberty".

Do NRMs have any place in the RE classroom? In the course of the research project on which this work is based many arguments for and against the use of any NRM were given.[5] The next section of this chapter will explore each of the different arguments and comment on their impact on the debate about NRMs and the RE classroom.

The case for

The number of adherents and community cohesion

When examining RE throughout England and Wales there seems to be an anomaly when comparing it with the religious makeup of society. Throughout the world, the six major religions in terms of membership numbers are the "big six". However in the United Kingdom there are more members of some individual NRMs than Buddhists.[6] This would suggest that NRMs may have a stronger case for inclusion within an RE classroom than some of the major world religions. If RE is to play a role in the fostering of community cohesion, then surely it should include some of the larger minority groups within UK society. This is supported by DCSF guidance on promoting cohesion issued by the DCSF where the communities that schools are encouraged to engage with are listed as: the school community; the community within which the school is located; the UK community; and the global community (2007: 5).

As examples of NRMs, Latter-day Saints and Jehovah's Witnesses highlight an interesting dichotomy. They want to be considered Christian, but consider themselves as groups distinct from the mainstream Christian churches. How can this tension be resolved? If these groups wish to be considered part of the Christian community then special mention in text books, agreed syllabuses and national documents is not always be possible within the curriculum time that is available for Christianity. If these groups are not seen as being in the main stream of Christianity, they may need special treatment or their needs for inclusion, understanding, and tolerance will not be met. In commissioning resources for use within the RE classroom, publishers tend to respond to the curriculum that is already in place rather than pushing the boundaries. NRMs may therefore not find themselves receiving coverage in resources. Specific resources that highlight the place of a particular NRM in light of "traditional" study would enable teachers to move forward with planning for their inclusion in the RE classroom.

A justification for including NRMs can be found in the recognition that a "major focus of RE is the study of diversity of religion and belief in the UK and how this influences national life" (DCSF, 2010: 8). One respondent to the research project noted that the case for the inclusion of NRMs in the RE classroom has not been coherently articulated (either as a whole or on an individual level). The respondent continued that "NRMs should take the power of their numbers to QCA and DCFS more effectively, and engage with RE – e.g. by joining the RE Council. The British Humanist Association provides a potential model for taking this forward effectively."

Every Child Matters

The non-statutory National Framework for RE does provide opportunity for the study of "a religious community with a significant local presence, where appropriate", and affirms that pupils should "express their own beliefs and ideas". (QCA, 2004: 27–28). RE which takes account of the individual child's religious experience can be advantageous for both pupil and teacher.

The interface between home and school life can sometimes be difficult for young people to negotiate. They deserve our best efforts as educationalists to ease their way. The presence in our schools of some individuals with clear religious views should be seen as an opportunity to share our common understanding and respect for each other on our overlapping journeys. Such contributions can enrich school life. (Gillespie in Redbridge SACRE, 1997: 4).

In 2001 Brunel University released an RE video resource called *Speaking for Ourselves*. This video "is made up of a wealth of testimony about the religious beliefs and practices of over fifty people with a variety of religious and ethnic identities. . . . Much of what they say concerns issues relating to personal, family and community life" (Lovelace, 2001: back cover). The video deals with the six principal religions, but also features a Humanist and a Jehovah's Witness. Including these groups could be seen to validate an individual child's religious experience. If it is not possible for each faith group to be represented, then allowing pupils an opportunity to speak for themselves and encounter the views of other classmates gives RE the opportunity to be more inclusive. These insights into children's world views can also be beneficial for the teacher. Bolton has also explained the benefits she sees in this kind of experience:

> If there are children from Pagan homes in the classroom, it is important for teachers to acknowledge and respect that. . . . One of the best ways is through getting to know a little about their faith, as I did when I taught my first Mormon student. He talked about the newly built Temple he attended and I managed to visit it, while it was open to the public before it was dedicated. This was a fascinating experience. (1999: 8–9)

It could be seen that an RE teacher is always learning; one of the arguments against the inclusion of NRMs outlined later in the chapter highlights subject knowledge as a barrier to teaching. Using the pupils themselves as a resource and also a teacher's engagement with that child's faith community can be seen to build the ability to teach about various groups. The use of individuals and small faith communities as a starting point for RE is building on the work that Jackson has done in developing the ethnographic approach to RE which emphasizes "listening to believers, insiders or adherents". It further highlights the "dynamism of religion in the life of the individual" (Blaylock, 2004: 13).

In the climate of today's schools where "Every Child Matters", listening to and valuing every child as an individual is crucial. If the RE classroom contains people from NRMs, then, it is crucial that they have a voice to explore and express their beliefs.

Examination of diversity

Within Christianity, for some issues, such as the use of legal drugs, there is no diversity except for personal application of principles (for example a Christian might decide to avoid the use of alcohol through personal choice and an interpretation of their body as a temple; but there tends to be no specific condemnation). However within the Church of Jesus Christ of Latter-day Saints there is a strict prohibition on tobacco, alcohol, and tea and coffee which could be explored in examining moral issues. Similarly, the treatment of Jehovah's Witnesses in the areas of war and medical issues could be seen to add greater diversity to the discussion. This addition of NRMs would add another dimension to the discussion and when answering exam questions give students more teachings on which to draw, and enable more students to reach the higher levels. For example AQA suggest that for the highest level in an AO1 question pupils should give "a full and coherent answer showing good development and/or analysis". For an AO2 question the relevance of differing points of view is recognized: "A well-argued response, with evidence of reasoned consideration of two different points of view showing informed insights and ability to apply knowledge and understanding of religion effectively" (AQA, 2008: 19).

Informing

Most teachers and pupils are unaware of the beliefs and teachings of NRMs. Miller (2004) discusses the centrality of the argument that RE is to be used to inform pupils of the beliefs and teachings of different religions:

> I'm convinced that RE has to move away from the "safe six" and be far more adventurous in what is included in RE – and NRMs are so much more obvious in society than some of the religions they study that we owe it to children to help them develop an informed understanding of Jehovah's Witnesses,

Latter-day Saints, Hare Krishnas and all the others they encounter – literally – on the streets.

In essence, the goal of informing underpins all the other arguments for the inclusion of NRMs in the RE classroom elucidated in this section. The arguments centre around the incorporation of groups who are increasing in size in the UK, and are bringing more and more children to the education system. As these children (as with all children) require an environment where they feel valued, and in which they and their culture matters, it would seem imperative that NRMs find their place in the RE classroom. Informing the general school population and enabling pupils to gain more enrichment through examination courses are laudable, but the most convincing argument seems to be the inclusion of children's own views. (On the other hand, this means that NRMs may not need to be covered equally thoroughly in all parts of the country.) This provisional conclusion will be challenged through the arguments suggested against the inclusion of NRMs. As the argument of this work is that NRMs should have a place in the RE classroom the ways in which these arguments can be overcome will also be explored.

The case against

In examining the arguments given by respondents against the incorporation of NRMs into the secondary RE curriculum there tended to be two families of concern. The first focusses on the problems associated with the practicalities of the subject as a whole, whilst the second focusses on the perceived dangers of NRMs.

The problems associated with the practicalities of the subject

When examining the demands placed upon RE in the classroom (lack of time and of specialist teachers, to mention only two) it may be argued that the requirement to balance the six major world religions (in various agreed syllabuses the number to be taught at KS3 ranges between three and six) is in itself a major challenge. To take the Manchester agreed syllabus (2003) as an example, the problem of curriculum space at Key Stage 3 is highlighted. Six principal religions are to be taught over an average of one hour per week. Finding time for further religions would place what could be seen as unreasonable demands on the curriculum and the teacher. If the teacher were to treat the NRMs as a part of the larger faith community then a study of them could be built into that unit of work. However the depth of study for the parent faith would be reduced substantially, especially in light of the above example where Christianity would receive approximately 13 hours of curriculum time.

It was suggested by one respondent that funding should be made available for RE libraries[7] which would contain a wider range of material than the syllabus topics, so that pupils could access information about NRMs. This would obviate the need to place further demands on the teacher and would enable pupils to become independent inquirers. However, this attempt to enable students to study religions depends on child motivation and interest. A similar argument could be suggested that if there is no time in geography lessons to study less economically developed countries, pupils could be directed towards the Internet and further resources.

Perhaps the solution to the concern about the practicalities of the subject is two-fold. First, the agreed syllabus Conferences could be less prescriptive in what is required in schools and give teachers an opportunity to respond to the interest of pupils, the religious make-up of the surrounding area or diversity in a religious tradition. This would localize RE to an even greater degree than agreed syllabuses already do and may not be a good thing. It would give teachers freedom but there is no guarantee that that freedom would be consistently applied. It might actually increase the burden on the teacher by unfairly extending their responsibility to include deciding and defending the content of RE.

The second solution to the practicalities of the subject could be the inclusion of NRMs in the secondary RE classroom as a "cherry picking" approach where aspects of the faiths are highlighted as appropriate. For example, as we saw earlier, in a discussion of war and peace the Jehovah's Witnesses' rejection of all participation in wars could be inserted as an alternative viewpoint. In Key Stage 3 in a study of rites of rassage initiation ceremonies from NRMs (especially those whose children are in the class/school) could be included. This would suggest that any slightly divergent teachings of NRMs (for example a belief that Jesus was crucified on a tree rather than on a cross) would not be touched upon as they could be seen to add little to the overall discussion of the parent faith.

Confusion

Teaching about NRMs could result in confusion. A respondent to the survey commented that pupils "at Key Stage 3 and Key Stage 4 are confused enough with the main (most populated) Christian denominations" (Respondent A). Certainly this seems to be a convincing argument. Children often mix up various aspects of the different traditions already studied and adding more would only deepen the confusion. However, confusion can result in studying any subject with varied (though similar) topics. As an example of this, one respondent compared his experience of teaching RE to his teaching of various psychological approaches at A Level. Students often mixed up the assumptions of the behaviourist with the biological approach. Confusion may be the natural result of studying more than one topic. Rather than seeing the study of NRMs as a negative imposition, it is possible to use the multiplicity of faiths as a positive aid to promote better learning. For example, a study of varying interpretations that could include NRMs could reach the higher levels of attainment:

> Level 7 . . . They explain why the consequences of belonging to a faith are not the same for all people within the same religion or tradition….
>
> Exceptional Performance . . . They provide a detailed analysis of how religious, spiritual and moral sources are interpreted in different ways, evaluating the principal methods by which religion and spirituality are studied. They synthesise effectively their accounts of the varied forms of religious, spiritual and moral expression. (QCA, 2004: 37).

Subject knowledge

A further argument against the use of NRMs in the secondary RE classroom is the lack of knowledge that a teacher may have about individual groups. Indeed, this is a valid concern based on the responses to the research project. In working with trainee teachers I have observed that it is rare to find an RE teacher who has qualified with a specialism in each of the six principal religions. However, it does not obviate the need for the individual teacher to study and experience more in order to fill in the gaps of their subject knowledge. If there is a pupil of a particular NRM in the school then they may well provide the teacher with opportunities to ask questions, or make links with communities to find information on which to build their study. For RE to be inclusive and perhaps follow the Life Themes approach to RE it needs to start being more "centred on the experiences of pupils in the RE classroom" (Blaylock, 2004a: 14) rather than the experience of the teacher. The fear that a lot of non-specialists have when they are teaching RE is that their subject knowledge will be insufficient. It is just the same for qualified RE teachers who need to be prepared to research.

The perceived dangers of NRMs

A major feature of NRMs is their perceived tendency to proselytize. If NRMs were to find a mention in the RE classroom it could lead to parental concern. NRMs are seen by some in the populist media to brainwash their adherents, though studies have argued that this accusation generally is not true (Barker, 1984; Barker, 2001).

One respondent suggested that NRMs should not be covered if "they are considered dangerous or manipulative to young people". Just as any good RE teaching involves shying away from a confessional approach (Grimmitt, 2000, does not recognize this as a valid apporachto the teaching of RE), this would be no less true for RE involving NRMs. The teaching of a NRM (or any religion) is not to promote acceptance, but rather for understanding of their truth claims; it should incorporate all pupils:

> truly educational teaching is directed to all pupils alike, since no distinction is made in divergent education between Christian pupils, Jewish pupils and pupils of no religious affiliation. . . . It does not mean that the teacher does not care but that he cares for them all, accepting them as they are. (Hull, 1984: 181)

As with any religion though, it is possible that a pupil's interest could be stimulated and they are then led to seek information for themselves. This leads on to another concern expressed by a respondent to the research project that teaching about NRMs might lead to a parent expressing their own fears and prejudices about the groups. This could lead to the consolidating of stereotypes and negative views. If the Unification Church were spoken of in response to topics in the RE class, how many of the parents would focus on brainwashing rather than the promotion of family unity? If the Latter-day Saints were discussed how many would speak of polygamy rather than helping and serving other people? There would need to be an atmosphere within the classroom where negative stereotypes could be challenged and prejudice erased. This would enable faiths to be approached without bias:

> Young people, as with all of us, recognise the difference between the authenticity of the individual voice and the rhetoric of ideological pronouncements. If we attend to the former and avoid the latter we shall gain their interest and engagement and advance their learning and development. (Erricker and Erricker, 2003: 204).

Conclusion

It would be wrong to dismiss NRMs from the teaching of RE because of parental and teacher prejudice, or in order to limit the scope of RE to areas in which the teacher is confident. The most persuasive argument against the inclusion of NRMs in the RE classroom is the great pressure that is already placed upon the RE curriculum. A cohesive phenomenological approach to individual religions may be seen to be the ideal by members of faith communities who are seeking parity with the major world religions.[8] Indeed, most adherents of a faith community would like to see their particular group given a curriculum block, where all aspects of belief and values could be explored in depth. However, with the great stresses already placed on the time given to RE, it isn't a realistic option to include every single faith group, NRM and/or denomination. My hope would be that diversity I explored and that the parent faith is not presented in a manner which isolates or excludes related NRMs. It would be incumbent on the teacher to identify the facets of NRMs that they felt could enhance the study of the parent faith. Although this may lead to accusations of "cherry picking", this may be unavoidable when faced with the demands of the RE curriculum in meeting the needs of local, national, and global communities in addition to those of the individual child.

The RE classroom should enable "pupils to develop respect for and sensitivity to others, in particular those whose faiths and beliefs are different from their own. It promotes discernment and enables pupils to combat prejudice" (QCA, 2004: 7).

The most persuasive argument for the inclusion of NRMs is in those environments where they may constitute the pupils' own world views. The good teacher builds upon the experiences of those pupils. The bad teacher would dismiss a child's faith as not relevant or else would have an erroneous understanding of that faith, upsetting and confusing the child and their family. However, when those children have been asked to share their beliefs, then increased understanding has come to both pupils and teachers. During the course of the research project a number of teachers explained how engaging with pupils about their faith had made the child feel valued while enhancing the teacher's knowledge. For some teachers the child and its parents may be the first members of a particular faith community that they have met. However, I would argue that NRMs shouldn't only be treated where there is a member of the faith present. Rather, teachers as a matter of course should seek for opportunities to include NRMs as appropriate. The fact that there are more Latter-day Saints or Jehovah's Witnesses in the UK than

Buddhists should suggest that there is a need that should be met.[9] It will not only add diversity to a discussion of Christianity (especially at Key Stage 4) but will prepare pupils to respect people from a myriad of faiths. This is the goal of any RE classroom, and should be extended to those whose faiths have a significant presence in the United Kingdom.

Having suggested that NRMs do have a valid place within the RE classroom this chapter will conclude with suggestions that may help this move forward.

The Way Forward

If NRMs are to find a place in the RE classroom then a variety of things need to take place.

NRMs need to involve themselves more in the RE world

As noted earlier, the case for the inclusion of individual NRMs has not been made convincingly. Thus NRMs could make their voices heard on committees such as the RE Council and on SACREs throughout the country. If NRMs would like to be on agreed syllabuses then they need to involve themselves in the committees that can make that happen.

If textbooks do not cover NRMs in any detail, the faith groups themselves could provide schools with material that could be used within the classroom. Even if such material is not used immediately, it would help to inform and prepare teachers. Resources with authentic voices would also help combat misrepresentation of these groups. Jehovah's Witnesses are an example of a group that publishes materials helping schools deal with issues that may arise with Witness pupils. Similarly, they have published the *Standing Firm* resource pack (Watch Tower, 1996), which helps teachers who have a desire and find it valuable to incorporate Jehovah's Witnesses into the teaching about the Holocaust. As with all resources, teachers using resources sent by NRMs would have to guard against propaganda.

Writers and curriculum developers who identify with a particular religious tradition have a special responsibility in representing religions. On the one hand, they have the advantage of the personal knowledge and experience of the insider (Jackson in Blaylock, 2004b: 7).

Suggesting that those who have a faith develop classroom materials is not as straightforward as it may seem. While not always practicable, the use of "faith insiders" and teachers to produce resources will be valuable for the RE teacher and the NRMs. Some groups may have people who meet both requirements, but a "faith insider" working with a serving teacher to develop resources will be as valuable. Providing information material would be of huge benefit to teachers, but practical resources would help serving teachers see where they could fit into existing schemes. Providing NRMs with a voice within the RE classroom and the RE world will only come from those with a vested interest – those within the communities themselves.

Teachers need to be open to learning about of the beliefs of NRMs

The practicalities of this need to be further explored. The possible resources that could be used include the Internet, faith communities themselves, training courses and publications. The problem with each of these (whether produced by NRMs or others) is the accuracy, bias, and propaganda that may be present. Certainly a search of the Internet on any of the NRMs will find both supportive and dismissive sites.

The possibility of a publication of a text book introducing the nature of NRMs may also be a helpful way forward. Although some already exist, most of them are not tailored to the needs of teachers; rather, they are written as specialist books to be found in university libraries, sometimes discussing the sociology and psychology of adherents rather than the beliefs and practices (e.g. Saliba, 1995). The problem with this suggestion is its practicality. What size of work would be needed to include all of those movements that demand attention? However, any work, no matter how limited in scope, would go a long way towards filling what presently is a large void in the RE world.

A training course involving NRMs as well as the principal religions would be very useful – education officers for NRMs could provide a viewpoint from their faith – though funding for teachers to attend would would constitute a fundamental problem in our present climate of very limited resourcing for R.E.

Certain positive steps are being taken. REsource have, in the last decade, published three articles that deal with NRMs (Holt, 2002,; Holt, 2003; Chryssides, 2003), but these are only small movements in the right direction. Much more needs to be done if teachers are to become aware of the place and practice of NRMs.

Pupils from NRMs need to be free and confident enough to share their beliefs as appropriate in lessons

The opportunity for pupils to discuss their beliefs and culture are fundamental in a supportive classroom. Pupils are valuable resources for the teaching of RE. If a topic links in with what the class are doing, then pupils should be free to discuss their perspective. For example, a Jehovah's Witness pupil might share their view on blood transfusions or war in their GCSE classroom (see Watch Tower, 1999).

For this to occur it will depend on pupil–teacher relations and also the confidence of the pupil themselves. If pupils feel they will be allowed to share their beliefs with no recriminations or derision, they are more likely to participate. It would also be incumbent on families and faith communities to provide the child with resources and help in presenting their views. This could also be supported by teachers, who, if they know about a child's faith, would be able to speak to them and ask them to share beliefs at appropriate times.

Conclusion

It is possible that the study of RE could continue without a mention of NRMs. However, this study would be greatly diversified and enhanced if these faiths were given an appropriate place within the classroom. At some point in our lives we will all encounter (or teach) a member of a NRM. Surely it is better to do so prepared with (even a basic) knowledge and understanding of what they believe. This would not only augment teachers' subject knowledge, but also further empower them in their pedagogical practice, engaging pupils, embracing and addressing their increasingly diverse needs, backgrounds and experiences and also promoting community cohesion with more breadth and depth.. The responsibility for taking up this opportunity lies as much with the NRM communities as with those responsible for the RE curriculum content and delivery.

Notes

1 The choice of these two NRMs is arbitrary and should not be taken to suggest that they are the only two faiths that should be studied. Indeed, the issues surrounding these two faiths may be replicated within other NRMs and provide interested parties with an opening to explore these other groups.

2 Barker (2001: 2) elucidates some of the characteristics that could be used to define New Religious Movements:

- The members are first generation converts.
- They tend to be atypical of society.
- There is often a founder or leader who wields charismatic authority – that is, he (or sometimes she) will be unbound by tradition or rules, but may be accorded by the followers the right to pronounce on all aspects of their life.
- There tends to be a far more clear cut version of "the truth" than in older religions, which have accommodated to generations throughout the ages.
- There is frequently a sharp distinction made by the group between "them" and "us", the former being homogeneously good and godly, the latter equally homogeneously bad and, perhaps, satanic.
- There is often (though not always) suspicion and/or antagonism from the wider society to which the group offers an alternative.

3 "In the process, both the academic and teacher will have gained in consistency by no longer paying lip service to a definition of New Religious Movement which does not correspond with their professional approach. If an appropriate definition is used, members of new religions are more likely to be reassured that they are being given fair treatment. As things stand, academics and anti-cultists are inclined to bend or ignore their professed definitions almost at will to suit their own purposes and this lack of consistency has caused considerable offence to a number of religious communities who, for example, have little wish to be bracketed together with 'Moonies' and Scientologists."

4 Barker, while arguing for first generation converts, does include Latter-day Saints as a NRM who do not meet this criterion.

5 These arguments were taken from a questionnaire that was given to approximately 100 secondary school teachers throughout England.

6 In the 2001 census 152,000 people (0.3%) identified themselves as Buddhist. The official Church figures available on www.lds.org for the Church of Jesus Christ of Latter-day Saints reports that there are 174,300 Latter-day Saints in the UK; it is unclear how many of the Latter-day Saints would identify themselves as active members – in the census most, if not all, Latter-day Saints will have ticked the Christian category. Jehovah's Witnesses at the end of 2003 reported on www.watchtower.org a UK membership of 124,828.

7 This assumes that the school library does not already have this type of resource available.

8 A phenomenological approach to RE suggests that religions are studied as a phenomenon "enabling pupils to get a firm grip on contours of religious studies" and individual religions (Blaylock, 2004: 13).

References

AQA. 2008. GCSE Religious Studies Specification A, Sample Assessment Materials.

Barker, E. 1984. *The Making of a Moonie: Brainwashing or Choice?* Oxford. Blackwell.

Barker, E. 2001. *An Introduction to New Religious Movements.* Lecture given at the Chaplaincy Centre, Imperial College London available at http://www.chaplaincy.ic.ac.uk/images/nrm_by_eb.pdf.

Blaylock, L. 2004a. 'Six Schools of Thought in RE', *Resource,* 27(1): 13–16.

Blaylock, L. (ed.). 2004b. *Representing Religions: Teachers of RE from Six Religions Explain how to Represent Their Religions in Your Classroom.* Birmingham. Christian Education.

Bolton, J. 1999. *An Investigation into the Place of Paganism within RE: A Teacher's Guide.* Farmington Fellows' Reports on Teaching and Training, TT33. Oxford. Farmington Institute.

Chryssides, G. 1994. 'New Religious Movements: Some Problems of Definition', *DISKUS International Journal of Religion* 2(2) available at http://www.uni-marburg.de/religionswissenschaft/journal/disku/chryssides.html.

Chryssides, G. 2003. 'Books on New Religious Movements', *REsource: The Journal of the Professional Council for Religious Education* 26(1): 4–7.

Derbyshire LEA. 2002. *Agreed Syllabus for Religious Education.*

DCSF. 2007. *Guidance on the Duty to Promote Community Cohesion.* London. Department for Children, Schools and Families.

DCSF. 2010. *Religious Education in English Schools: Non-statutory Guidance 2010.* Nottingham. Department for Children, Schools and Families.

Erricker, C., and Erricker, J. 2003. 'The Children and Worldviews Project: A Narrative Pedagogy of Religious Education', in Grimmitt, M. (ed.) *Pedagogies of Religious Education: Case Studies in the Research and Development of Good Pedagogic Practice in RE.* Great Wakering. McCrimmons: 188–206.

Grimmitt, M. (ed.). 2000. *Pedagogies of Religious Education.* Great Wakering. McCrimmons.

Holt, J.D. 2002. 'The Church of Jesus Christ of Latter-day Saints in the RE Classroom', *REsource: The Journal of the Professional Council for Religious Education* 24(3): 6–8.

Holt, J.D. 2004. 'Jehovah's Witnesses in the RE Classroom', *REsource: The Journal of the Professional Council for Religious Education* 26(2): 617–619.

Hull, J. 1984. *Studies in Religion and Education.* London. Falmer.

Lovelace, A. 2005. *Speaking for Ourselves.* [DVD.] Norwich. RMEP.

Manchester LEA. 2003. *The Agreed Syllabus for Religious Education.* Manchester. Manchester LEA.

Miller, J. 2004. Email to author, 25 May 2004.

Nottinghamshire County Council. 2003. *Nottinghamshire Agreed Syllabus for Religious Education.* Nottinghamshire County Council.

Partridge, C. (ed.) 2004. *Encyclopedia of New Religions: New Religious Movements, Sects and Alternative Spiritualities.* Oxford. Lion.

QCA. 2004. *Religious Education: The Non-Statutory National Framework.* London. Qualifications and Curriculum Authority.

Redbridge SACRE. 1997. *Jehovah's Witnesses and the School.* London Borough of Redbridge.

Saliba, J.A. 1995. *Perspectives on New Religious Movements.* London: Geoffrey Chapman.

Watch Tower. 1996. *Jehovah's Witnesses Stand Firm Against Nazi Assault.* [Videocassette.] 1996. NY. Watch Tower Bible and Tract Society.

Watch Tower. 1999. *How Blood Can Save Your Life.* NY. Watch Tower Bible and Tract Society.

Weller, P. (ed.) 1997. *Religions in the UK: A Multi-Faith Directory.* 2nd ed. Derby. University of Derby.

Wilson, B.R. 1993. 'The Persistence of Sects', *DISKUS* 1(2): 1–12 available at http://www.uni-marburg.de/religionswissenschaft/journal/diskus/wilson.html.

Wintersgill, B. 1993. 'Learning about World Religions in the Basic Curriculum', in Erricker, C. (ed.) *Teaching World Religions: A Teacher's Handbook produced by the SHAP Working Party on World Religions in Education.* London. Heinemann: 42–44.

Chapter Six

Engagement and the Religious Education Curriculum: Perspectives from Feminist Theology

Gaynor Pollard

In common with many educational initiatives such as *Excellence and Enjoyment* (DfES, 2003), engagement is an activity without a subject. Our students are to be encouraged to engage with their study as a primary activity. If the content of the lesson does not appear to be engaging them then a different methodology must be used. We can engage them creatively, using active methods, spiritually, by appealing to their emotional intelligence, visually, through film and art; we can wire them up globally so that they can visit religious sites across the world, we can ask them to begin journeys of personal reflection so that they become the centre of the study, and may concentrate on their own development as a range of phenomena and ideas are presented to them. Any flagging of engagement means that ever more imaginative pedagogies must be attempted.

Central to all these approaches is an underlying philosophy of individualism. Engagement begins with the individual, carving a way through attractively presented information. Our students are used to moving around virtual universes quickly, and to changing the canvas when they encounter difficulty. With the world as their playground, for them to become engaged with a particular area there must be a return for their effort, and that return is normally measured in enjoyment. Engagement becomes a response to the amount of enjoyment available.

This emphasis on individualism, the "turn to the self", is a particular challenge for traditional religions, where the emphasis has always lain upon self-forgetfulness, self-discipline, submission to a greater authority, selfless service to others, fortitude in the face of suffering, and a certain amount of fearfulness in the face of the divine. To engage students with these areas is to recall them to theologies of former times. It is true that, in a paradoxical way, those religions that fare best in terms of engaging numbers of believers are those that offer traditional teaching and organization: monolithic systems that rely upon an authoritative approach, clear moral guidance, and membership that depends upon conformity to a pre-formed system. It is not that these religions *present* themselves as reactionary and backward looking: on the contrary, they are often early adopters of new technology. However the *content* of the religion remains traditional even if it is delivered via an Ipod app or an RSS feed.

Despite the success of these groups, engagement is something that seems to be eluding Christian churches. Even taking account of the growth in numbers in the more conservative religious groups, overall the number of people with formal connections to the Christian faith is in drastic decline in the West, a development that is expected to continue (Heelas and Woodhead, 2005).

It is clear that young people in our schools are following this trend. Nevertheless the content of the subject remains traditional, based on definitions of each religion approved by their own leaders. Contemporary approaches in the classroom rely on imaginative and inspired productions, written, choreographed, and directed by religious education teachers, using the best of the available technology. The teachers' efforts are expended in the cause of presenting content that is similar to anything that might have been taught in schools 50 years ago. In the music industry this method makes its appearance as a cover version, where original songs are re-released with enhanced production. When the quality of the original work is clear, each new incarnation brings added commercial success. The comparison between the music industry and religious education breaks down with the realization that the music industry introduces new work alongside its covers. New voices are heard, new ethnic music is celebrated, and the gems of the past are integrated alongside contemporary offerings.

In religious education it is extraordinarily difficult to encourage syllabus writers to consider new material. Conveying information about religions is one of the primary rationales offered for teaching religious education in maintained schools. What is a lot less transparent is the rationale for the selection of information, whose version is privileged, and how the information itself may be understood with integrity by both insiders and outsiders of the faith communities.

At first sight it might appear that religious education professionals have a unique opportunity to take responsibility for the content of their syllabuses. In England and Wales it is maintained and monitored locally by a variety of groups that contain leading members of the religious traditions, local councillors, and teachers. This process seems to ensure a highly democratic process of curriculum development, where the constituent members appear to ensure diversity, in a way that is not required in the formulation of the National Curriculum. In fact, this apparent inclusiveness cloaks the suppression of dissidence and diversity within the religious communities themselves. This raises questions for the religious education of children and young people, including the extent of the responsibility of the school to support the beliefs and values of local faith communities, when these are by no means agreed within the communities themselves.

Those schools whose local authorities have been influenced by the National Framework for Religious Education follow the two attainment targets, "Learning About Religion" and "Learning From Religion", and as a rule limit their selection of content to six major traditions (QCA, 2004). This selection appears to be entirely reasonable, for two main reasons. First, the selection of content has been achieved through a consensus among what most would consider the major players, including parents, teachers, and the faith communities themselves. This is no mean feat, as an examination of religious education in other parts of the world would show. In many countries religious education, by reason of its controversial nature, is either excluded from the curriculum altogether, or taught in faith groups by agencies external to the school (Brown, 1992: 27). Additionally the diverse manifestations of religious belief are so varied and complex that it makes sense to limit the study to those religions that have the largest following in England and Wales. Nevertheless the consensus method of choosing content has been subject to some criticism:

> Ever since the early 1960s Religious Education's place within the modern education system has been equivocal. The plurality of religious traditions, coupled with secular suspicion of religion, led to charges of indoctrination and doubts whether the subject could justify its place within an open liberal educational context. This resulted in a curriculum development programme driven primarily by the desire to achieve public consensus at the expense of any recognition of the diversity and ambiguity of religion. (Wright, 1999: 27)

By its very nature consensus often involves a compromise that is always going to be less than satisfactory, but may nevertheless aim to be the best that is available. However, it is clear that, in making decisions about content, much material will be excluded. There needs to be a resolve not to foreclose on the debate about which religious traditions and which strands of those traditions should be studied, but instead to keep the position under review. Significant spiritual insights and religious convictions tend to spring from unlikely sources and surprising contexts. To fix the canon of religious education at any stage is to impose a false coherence in the areas of beliefs and values. This raises the question of why content needs to be stipulated at all, and whether agreed syllabuses might concern themselves instead with outlining pedagogies that would prove suitable for achieving the aims of the subject. This would leave teachers free to introduce examples of their own choosing, appropriate to the local situation. Instead syllabuses have developed into detailed specifications of content, often with only brief guidance about how it might be delivered.

The question of which traditions within the religion are being studied is very rarely asked. It is taken for granted by most teachers that the faith groups that contributed to the syllabus have provided an unambiguous account of the religion in question. Diversity within Christianity is represented in the presentation of a variety of denominations who demonstrate different but amiably collegiate ways of living a Christian life, rather than diversity as controversy, uncertainty, accompanied by often painful internal critique amongst believers of all groups. This is unsurprising when the selection of material for teaching about religions has been the preserve of groups screened carefully for their traditional orthodoxy. Minority beliefs and practices stand little chance of representation.

Hull has reflected upon the criteria for the selection of content in religious education (Hull, 1992). He critiques the current practice of forming syllabuses about the Christian religion on three grounds. Statements of faith tend to be heavily doctrinal and are often rooted in a different historical context. Such summaries tend to be directed either towards teaching the faithful or justifying the existence of the denomination. Finally, with the huge number of denominations present within Christianity, the job appears to be undoable (Hull, 1992: 4). He suggests, instead, that a single-discipline approach might be employed, whereby Christianity might be offered, say, within an historical perspective. He offers the example of a progressive scheme where Key Stage 1 could be based on narrative Christianity, Key Stages 2 and 3 on historical Christianity, and Key Stage 4 on philosophical and ethical Christianity (Hull, 1992: 5). Another version of this might be to confine the study to early historical origins, whereby some "classical essence" of the faith could be identified and explored. This would involve study of the Bible as a normative expression of the faith (Hull, 1992: 6). He suggests a further approach involving the study of Christianity in its contemporary forms approached, for example, through theatre or film, supported by the discipline of ethnography (Hull, 1992: 7).

This careful and considered work, opening up the debate for genuine consideration, is offered in a spirit of irony, since Hull knows that the important issues are neither social nor educational, although they ought to be:

> It is important to realise that the curriculum discussions about an appropriate method for the teaching of Christianity, whether it should be taught through themes and topics, whether it should be taught experientially or phenomenologically, whether it should be taught with other faiths or in isolation from them, are only superficially to be regarded as questions of religious education method. It is deeper than that. They are symptoms of different perspectives regarding the character of Christianity. The problem of curriculum selection in Christianity is not only educational; it is theological. (Hull, 1992: 7)

The most powerful Christian groups in the political arena will be able to control content and, with that, will be able to define the faith for educational purposes on theological grounds. Curriculum selection on theological grounds in Christianity works from a "classical essence" which has already silenced diversity. In particular selection is made from a store of traditions in which women and girls are largely invisible, and the major contribution of Christian feminist theologians has been overlooked.

The question of gender bias in religious education in the UK began to be examined in the 1980s (Trevett, 1983). As early as 1979 Roman Catholic bishops in the USA were encouraging attention to this aspect in religious education.

> A woman who views herself as the image of God is conscious of her great dignity, a dignity which bestows self acceptance and self esteem. Wherever, within the church or society, a woman does not find liturgies, educational programmes, social events or decision-making structures which meet her own and others' needs, she should work with persistence to establish them. (The Roman Catholic Bishops of Minnesota, 1979: 11)

This early trend lost ground very quickly. Higgins presented strong evidence for bias against women in his analysis of Church of England Diocesan syllabuses of religious education. He found instances of exclusive language when referring to the Christian community, and the equating of family domestic roles with the work of women across a range of guidelines. The Sheffield scheme tackled Mothering Sunday with a picture of the mother in question washing up. Higgins' survey revealed that the Canterbury and Rochester scheme addressed the question of gender stereotyping in its secondary material, but still managed to mention only two women, Eve and Bathsheba, in its 76 pages of notes and comments on the teaching of the Bible. In the Winchester scheme in the outline for the Church of England there was mention of 23 men and "the Pilgrim Fathers", and one woman, Florence Nightingale. Manchester mentioned 12 men but no women (Higgins, 1998).

Similarly, despite the fact that Roman Catholic women have been in the forefront of developments in feminist theology, both in the UK and in the United States, little progress was made in applying these principles to religious education in Roman Catholic schools. Hallows for her analysis of Roman Catholic guidelines used a fourfold typology of sexism by exclusion or omission, by subordination, by distortion, and by degradation. Her findings were similar to Higgins, in that she found little or no attempt to use inclusive language and an overwhelming use of male exemplars in biblical studies and in the history of the Church. Sexism by subordination was found in Mary's image, which was presented as domestic and maternal, rather than courageous and educative. Sexism by distortion is particularly important in the selection of biblical material, since those women who are portrayed in syllabuses are often chosen for their sinfulness. Hallows was particularly disturbed by examples of sexism by degradation, where exemplar material presents men involved in powerful activities (business meetings), and women concerned with the trivial (coffee mornings) (Hallows, 1998).

Thatcher places the blame squarely on Church authorities:

> What use is the *imprimatur* from faith communities of RE syllabuses and teaching materials in the schools of the world, in helping to combat gender inequality, if the authorisers are themselves gender-insensitive? (Thatcher, 1999: 66)

Engagement in religious education involves presenting material that has a clear relevance to the students. If 50% of the students find their gender under-represented at best, and completely invisible at worst, then there is little chance that they will involve themselves wholeheartedly in the study, yet they will find very little support from the patriarchal leaders of religions. An example from religious language illustrates the dilemma. Those who relate to feminine imagery of God are hard pressed to find their perspective represented in religious education. Many feminist theologians have argued that traditional names for God are often alienating for women: "Words such as Everlasting Father, Mighty King, Prince of Peace express images of God that create distance between women and God" (Blair, 1992: 535).

In contrast to these powerfully patriarchal images, many Christians have enjoyed songs celebrating Washerwoman God, Widow Woman God, and Bag Lady God (Wren, 1980: 169–70). McFague carries the argument further by pointing out that God-language expressed in metaphors carries meaning in two directions, so that God the Father may tell us about God, but it also tells us about the fathers, in that they become more closely equated with God, and those who are not the fathers are seen as ungodly (McFague, 1982: 147–152).

Raphael, working within a Jewish context, is able to make an erudite case for naming God using feminine terms, but recognizes that there are overwhelming factors that prevent such religious views gaining a place on the curriculum:

> Neither Orthodox Jews nor all non-Orthodox Jews would accept that feminist theological (let alone theological) imagery for God is a legitimate part of Judaism. This places the feminist teacher in something of a dilemma. She or he may at once subscribe to the reputable ideal of non-confessional, non-indoctrinatory RE but may also wish to attend truthfully to the effects of patriarchal religious views on children (especially, but not exclusively, on the self-image and understanding of girls). In other words, criticism of religion can hardly be ethically avoided where there is critical attention to the role of gender in religion. (Raphael, 1999: 77)

Teachers who have been introduced to feminist theologies are troubled by this dilemma, and receive little support from the statutory authorities or from faith groups in their attempt to deal with the issues with integrity. Strategies to deal with diversity have included on the one hand packing the curriculum with the detail that might do justice to the range of belief and practice within a religion, and on the other, using the religion instrumentally, in order to serve the needs of the child (Grove, 2005: 4). In the first case this would mean including reams of information that many believers would find peripheral to their faith and, in the second, privileging the students' need for relevant material about women and girls so that the religions are presented in a way that does not do justice to their history. Instead Grove suggests that it is possible to avoid both these extremes by concentrating on single, specific items:

> The more specific the item, the greater and more immediate the impact: the kara rather than the five Ks, Balkrishna instead of "Babies", or this particular bible with its history, rather than the Bible generally. (Grove: 2005: 5)

Presenting a specific Christian hymn or prayer that addresses God as Mother, or a female image of God, enables discussion and reflection to take place without denying the reality of a tradition that, in the main, relates to God as male.

The inclusion of women and girls in religious discussion may also be addressed through biblical texts where there is a range of work to draw from in feminist biblical exegesis. Hanlon characterizes feminist approaches as reforming, rejecting, replicating, and transforming. Reform theologians accept scriptural authority as "feminist in intent". Effort is made to rediscover women's "lost" history and liberate the original, "authentic" message. Liberationist, radical, and socialist perspectives believe biblical texts to be overtly patriarchal and male-centred, and that women have been intentionally "written out" of the scriptures. Women's voices must be reclaimed as authoritative in themselves (Hanlon, 2002: 127). Upton detects three main approaches derived from feminist apologetic responses to patriarchal argument (Upton, 2002: 98). The first can be found in the work of Rosemary Radford Ruether, where a tradition of liberation is traced from the Exodus through to the New Testament. The texts which deal directly with liberation of the oppressed become "a canon within a canon", and the norm by which all other biblical texts are judged (Ruether, 1998). The second approach is typified by Phyllis Trible, where an attempt is made to retrieve texts which have been overlooked or distorted by patriarchal hermeneutics (Trible, 1984). The third approach is to revise the present canon, so that biblical traditions can show that the historical situation allowed a greater role for women than the codified texts suggest. This method involves studying canonical texts in order to unpack more detail about the women who appear there, and searching non-canonical heterodox second- and third-century texts for hidden clues to the function of women in early Christian communities. Using this method MacKenzie suggests some new approaches involving feminist iconography. Women in the Bible must be depicted as subjects in their own right, rather than as background images for the male hero. Conversely the lives of men in the Bible might be understood in terms of women's journeys and be related to women's experience. Genre pictures should be introduced, depicting everyday life in a way that is not idealized (MacKenzie, 1995: 10, 13). These reversals would serve the purpose of shocking the observer into new ways of thinking and experiencing the lives of biblical women and also, perhaps, their own. All these approaches could be addressed in religious education.

Upton explores the feminist preference for narrative models, first as a reaction to historical critical methods but, more importantly, as a method of showing respect for the majority of biblical genres. This allows a study of narrative elements such as tempo, plot, and characterization. Studies have been made of the women in Mark's Gospel, for example, or the hidden women in Judges, focussing not just on depictions favourable to women but on those which show the abusive nature of some texts in their treatment of the women who appear there (Upton, 2002: 103–104). The crucial question for women of faith has been how to make the link between story and scripture, between history and sacred text. The answer provided by women's Bible studies is that texts must be explored through imagination and ritual (Blair, 1992: 542). Plaskow suggests: "Information about women's pasts may be instructive and even stirring, but it is not transformative until it becomes part of the community's collective memory" (Plaskow, 1989: 44), and suggests the use of midrash to facilitate this process.

Using narrative to provide opportunities for reflection and learning is a common method in schools, and encouraging teachers to use skills more usually connected with literacy could prompt pupils to engage with biblical material in a way that enables them to bring their own experiences and contexts to bear. Methods of encouraging pupils to become biblical theologians, active in interpretation and application, would do better justice not only to the pupils' experience, but also to the Bible itself. Althaus-Reid reminds us of the dynamic character of the text: "such is the Bible, which is the memory of the praxis of the Word" (Althaus-Reid, 2004: 65).

The "praxis of the Word" is exactly what is not encouraged in schools, in the name of neutrality. Consideration of different ways of being remain cognitive activities, and the expression of beliefs through actions is regarded as far too political and controversial to be advocated in the educational environment. An analysis of the biblical text in terms of its present applicability rather than in its past meanings might provide a way of approaching biblical studies in religious education which would enable present well-being for all to be a primary concern. This approach finds some support from Kay, who researched the ways in which Christianity was presented in examination syllabuses. His main conclusion was that Christianity would be better served if study began in the present and worked backwards, rather than the other way round (Kay, 1999). Although he is referring to the churches' life in the present, it would only need one further step in this direction to begin with the experience of the pupils.

If this agenda were pursued, the place of women and all other peoples who have been marginalized in biblical hermeneutics, and therefore also in the school curriculum, might be recovered. In any case, attention would shift from authoritative readings to the reader herself. The work of the Biblos project, undertaken by the University of Exeter School of Education in association with the Bible Society, has shown that it is possible to enable pupils to learn the skills of "faithful interpretation and transforming enactment", where "faithful" means remaining faithful to personal experience and understanding, rather than to an authoritative and non-negotiable hermeneutic. The process has the advantage of authenticity and integrity, and provides an opportunity for all voices to be heard. When the pupils articulate their own responses they are able to build the confidence they need to critique both their own opinions and the opinions of others. These critiques would include a rigorous examination of mainstream religious teachings, and also alternative perspectives. The Biblos project undertook this research to establish attitudes to Bible teaching in Key Stages 2 and 3 and to develop and evaluate new methodologies (Copley and Savini, 1998). The research, undertaken in Ealing and Devon, used three key themes of Destiny, Encounter, and Vulnerability and was planned to bridge the gap between the text and the experience of pupils. It expressly avoided using technical theological language such as atonement, covenant, and sacrifice. The findings of the project suggest that teacher support materials were more important than pupil textbooks in supporting effective biblical teaching. Additionally and significantly they made this suggestion:

> Bible understanding has replaced Bible knowledge as a key aim. We want children not to half-digest the theology of others, but to start to theologise for themselves. (Copley and Savini, 1998)

The method is a reversal of the traditional method of listening to a biblical story, absorbing the traditional interpretation (since there is almost always only one on offer), writing it down in your own words and possibly drawing a picture. Instead the requirement is that each student becomes a biblical theologian, drawing on their own experience, their personal encounter with the text, and only then beginning to consider the interpretations of others. It is a method that has been previously employed by liberation theologians to acquire some control of their own theological learning and political agency. Religious education as theologizing suggests that *context,* in this case the context of the students, is the beginning of religious education. Since at least half of those studying are girls, this would suggest that there is room here for taking the experience of girls and women seriously, an area almost completely neglected in previous biblical work in schools.

Krisman has made some important observations about religious education and special needs that speak clearly for the view that all voices have validity. She begins by reviewing and critiquing the approaches and activities that are recommended in special needs contexts, which have typically been based upon a deficit model, and cites examples of classroom practice such as the reading of the parable of the lost sheep, followed by feeling wool, visiting a farm and making a sheep mask, which may prepare the pupils in terms of their experience of the world, but does not allow them to explore religious issues in any meaningful way (Krisman, 1999: 7). She draws from her own experience in presenting the parable of the prodigal son to her special needs Year 9 class. Encouraged to engage personally with the text, the overwhelming reaction was that the story was one of bereavement or divorce. The pupils felt that the central character, the missing mother, would have changed the whole course of events. This interpretation is a long way from the traditional Christian interpretation of the Father God, endlessly forgiving and accepting the returning sinner, but it opens up a whole new line of theological inquiry about responsibility on the part of the prodigal son, damaged by loss, the father, who might have known better than to release huge resources to a young man, and the way in which a patriarchal religion, where questioning of the actions of the father are unthinkable, lacks the figure of the mother which would have changed the story completely. The insights of a special needs class have their place in biblical hermeneutics.

More pioneering work has been undertaken in prioritizing the voices of the pupils and students. O'Grady, faced with a dip in motivation in Year 8 students, decided that the students' own ideas and experiences should be valued equally with material from religious traditions. As well as presenting them with a scheme of work, he asked the class what else they would like to learn (O'Grady, 2003: 216–217). It seems astonishing that this is an unusual practice, yet the bureaucratization of education in England and Wales has led to an unwillingness among teachers to depart from the published scheme. In addition to inviting comments about the content of the study, O'Grady also asked for input on which related questions about life they would like to investigate, which methods of work they would prefer, and how the work could be made harder and more interesting than Year 7 work. These are modest beginnings, but O'Grady was able to report a significant difference in the engagement of the students.

Doing theology can be a dynamic, contemporary, and social process. Hunt articulates the movement towards this method amongst Christian feminist theologians:

> Today the function of theology is to be a process, not a product. It is an organic and communal, participator process through which people of a common faith share insights, stories and reflections on questions of ultimate meaning and value. (Hunt, 2000: 11)

A curriculum which begins with the students' reaction to religious belief and practice is already developing in some parts of Europe (Iversen, 2009). The activities of theologizing and philosophizing demand engagement from students in a way that privileging the learning of others never could. Clearly these new methods and theologies cannot be applied in religious education using curriculum content that has been appropriated uncritically from patriarchal religious traditions. The relationship between the state, local education authorities, and the religious communities in the production of agreed syllabuses and Diocesan Guidelines means that the content of religious education is almost invariably taken from the mainstream and the conservative tradition of religious thought and practice. There are many who believe that education in these traditions has served our children well, but increasingly voices of protest may be heard:

> Patriarchy, with its dominance and submission dynamics, is a barrier to an interdependence and mutuality that can guide the vision of a holistic and egalitarian society in multiple ways. It limits the capacity of society to call forth the gifts of women. It also brings needless suffering into the lives of men of color for reasons that are part of patriarchy's history. But not only are men and women of color deprived of opportunities for developing and expressing their gifts, white men are also deprived of the gifts of both groups and of developing their own in relationship to them. The androcentrism that accompanies patriarchy sentences men to a myopia that sees the white male point of view to be the only view of a situation. When this is the case, every group is diminished. (Clifford, 2001: 21)

Applying theology to religious education is difficult within a discipline that takes Religious Studies as its starting point. It might be argued that internal confrontations expressed by feminist theologians need have no effect upon religious education, who must teach the mainstream as they find it. It is, however, becoming increasingly clear that the methodologies of Religious Studies also suffer from partiality and bias:

> The sources, concepts, models and theories of religious studies are male-derived and male-centred; they operate with a generic masculine which implies that men have almost always spoken for and about women. (King, 2000: 19)

If we expect students to engage with religious traditions, we must take their own perspectives seriously. We must allow for diversity *within* each tradition, not just *between* them. Teachers are powerfully influenced by the desire to avoid offence, and often direct this deference towards the leaders of the religious traditions. Since the leaders are almost always men, and almost always chosen for their conservative and traditional attitudes, acceptable classroom material is almost certain to reflect the mainstream patriarchal power centres. As the numbers of formal followers decline, theological reflection is taking place outside the traditional centres of power (Davie, 1994). During the next years we can continue to limit ourselves to learning about religions or we can open up our classrooms to the process of theological reflection, drawing on an eclectic range of ideas, movements, and perspectives. The world is a complex mixture of competing beliefs and ideologies, and it is this world for which teachers prepare students. Examination of the unorthodox will allow young people to develop the skills they will need, if they are to avoid a future in which dissenters are burnt at the stake. Dissent has a long and distinguished history in Christianity. It has enabled the worse excesses of Christian practice to be challenged and has launched countless reform movements to counter corrupt practices. Even when the teaching of the dissenters themselves has been of dubious moral value, it has served the purpose of causing the dominant tradition to defend itself in creative and innovative ways. In the two thousand year history of Christianity the Church as an institution has had to adapt, reformulate, rise to encounter new situations and listen to its critics. Without the critical spirit within its ranks it would fossilize in a past age, no longer able to respond to the swift pace of change inherent in the contemporary situation. In school-based religious education, however, we are not dealing with dissent *within* the ranks, as alternatives to dominant traditions. It is not the purpose of religious education to reform churches; although this might be an outcome, it would not be an intentional one. Appropriate educational responses to diverse beliefs must include vigilance in enabling criticism, the flowering of new spiritualities, and the exploration of new possibilities in religious thinking. With the decline in church attendance, many of these possibilities will be available to children within the context of the school or not at all. Religious education must seek to enable, not only the acquiring of information about religion, but also the practice of skills which will enable religious claims and practices to be subject to committed debate. The answers to religious inquiries should not be allowed to be patented by conventional religious believers alone. For many teachers the possibility of causing offence to believers is one that fills them with trepidation, and they would prefer to avoid all areas that might prove controversial. However, with religious controversy often erupting into full scale war, and with every possibility that this will continue in the future, if young people are shielded from controversial issues then they will find themselves as poorly equipped as past generations to cope with the suffering that clashes of religious ideologies can produce. Students must be educated to hone the skills they will need to challenge religious metanarratives, when these prove inadequate to new situations, and also to recognise a traditional wisdom when it proves its worth. Now that is a task worth engaging with.

References

Althaus-Reid, M. 2004. *From Feminist Theology to Indecent Theology*. London. SCM Press.

Blair, C.E. 1992. 'Women's Spirituality Empowered by Biblical Story', *Religious Education,* 87(4).

Brown, A. 1992. 'Religious Education in Europe', *RE Today.*

Clément, C. 2002. 'Foreword' in Joy, M. et al. (eds.). *French Feminists on Religion: A Reader.* London. Routledge.

Clifford, A.M. 2001. *Introducing Feminist Theology*. Maryknoll, NY. Orbis.

Copley, T., and Savini, H. 1998. 'The State of the Bible in State Schools', *Transmission*.

Davie, G. 1994. *Religion in Britain Since 1945: Believing Without Belonging.* Oxford. Blackwell.

DfES. 2003. *Excellence and Enjoyment: A Sstrategy for Primary Schools.* London. Department for Education and Skills.

Grove, J. 2005. 'A Gift . . . Revisited', *REsource,* 28(1).

Hallows, C. 1998. 'Sexism and Religious Education in Roman Catholic Schools', *Digest*. Association of Christian Teachers.

Hanlon, D. 2002. 'Not "either-or", more a case of "both-and": Towards an Inclusive Gender Strategy for Religious Education', in Broadbent, L., and Brown, A. (eds.). *Issues in Religious Education*. Abingdon. Routledge.

Heelas, P., and Woodhead, L. 2005. *The Spiritual Revolution: Why Religion is Giving Way to Spirituality.* Oxford. Blackwell.

Higgins, J. 1998. 'Gender and Church of England Diocesan Syllabuses of Religious Education', *Digest*. Association of Christian Teachers.

Hull, J.M. 1992. 'Editorial: Christianity in Religious Education', *British Journal of Religious Education*, 15(1).

Hunt, M.E. 2000. 'Feminist Theo-Politics: Religions and Power', *Feminist Theology* 25.

Iversen, Y. et al. (eds.). 2009. *Hovering over the Face of the Deep: Philosophy and Theology with Children*. Münster. Waxmann.

Kay, W. 1999. 'Can World Religions in the Secondary School be Counter Productive?', *Digest* 26(1). Association of Christian Teachers.

King, U. 2000. 'Introduction: Gender and the Study of Religion', in King, U. (ed.). *Religion and Gender*. 2nd ed. Oxford. Blackwell.

Krisman, A. 1999. 'Building up to the Sky', *REsource* 21(2).

McFague, S. 1982. *Metaphorical Theology*. Philadelphia, PA .Fortress Press.

MacKenzie, C. 1995. 'Liberation and Imagination: Art, Theology and Women's Experience', *Feminist Theology* 8.
O'Grady, K. 2003. 'Motivation in Religious Education: A Collaborative Investigation with Year Eight Students', *British Journal of Religious Education*, 25(3).
Plaskow, J. 1989. 'Jewish Memory from a Feminist Perspective', in Plaskow, J. et al. (eds.). *Weaving the Visions: New Patterns in Feminist Spirituality*. San Francisco. Harper & Row.
QCA. 2004. *National Framework for Religious Education*. London. Qualifications and Curriculum Authority.
Raphael, M. 1999. '"I Will Be Who I Will Be": The Representation of God in Postmodern Jewish Feminist Theology and Contemporary Religious Education', *British Journal of Religious Education* 21(2).
Roman Catholic Bishops of Minnesota. 1979. *Woman: Pastoral Reflections*. St Paul, MN.
Ruether, R.R. 1998. *Women and Redemption: a Theological History*. London. SCM Press.
Thatcher, A. 1999. 'Editorial: Religious Education and Gender', *British Journal of Religious Education* 21(2).
Trevett, C. 1983. 'The Lady Vanishes', *British Journal of Religious Education* 15(2).
Trible, P. 1984. Texts of Terror. London, SCM Press.
Upton, B.G. 2002. 'Feminist Theology as Biblical Hermeneutics', in Parsons, S.F. (ed.). *The Cambridge Companion to Feminist Theology*. Cambridge. Cambridge University Press.
Wren, B. 1980. *What Language Shall I Borrow? God-Talk in Worship: a Male Response to Feminist Theology*. New York. Paulist Press.
Wright, A. 1999. *Spiritual Pedagogy: A Survey, Critique and Reconstruction of Contemporary Spiritual Education in England and Wales*. Culham. Culham College Institute.

Chapter Seven

Philosophy with Teenagers: Nurturing a Moral Imagination for the Twenty-first Century, or, Why We Need an Inquiry Based Pedagogy for Religious Education in the Secondary School

Patricia Hannam

The aim of this chapter is to outline an argument as to why inquiry should form the central principle for religious education in a plural democracy. In the light of increasing globalization I go on to suggest, albeit tentatively, that such an "inquiry focussed" religious education will contribute to the nurture of a moral imagination fit for our current moment in history.

We live in uncertain times. Following a period of mass globalization which has impacted on several generations of young people in the UK today, there is a sense of grave insecurity on many levels. By globalization I mean, in part, the steady decline in importance of national boundaries and geographical distance as constraints on mobility. The impact of this increased mobility can be seen in a great many ways, some positive and others less so. In addition, since World War Two there has been the rebuilding of the global economy around a deliberate and structural consumerism: people, goods and services, factors of production and their owners, financial capital, enterprises, technology, brand names, knowledge, ideas, culture, and values: all these things now move with increasing ease across national frontiers. As products and services have moved so have people and belief systems.

The negative aspects of globalization, such as a rise in whole communities living in poverty, include the international spread of contagious diseases which accompany the increased mobility of humans and animals. Today, TB, HIV-AIDS, Ebola virus, Nile virus and flu virus can spread with alarming speed. Crime (the drugs trade, money laundering, and tax evasion) has become a global industry. There are shadowy links between our international financial systems and much criminal behaviour. The unbounded consumption by a small part of the world's population has led to immense suffering elsewhere. Perhaps even more significant is the complex web of environmental destruction. The links are subtle and require intelligent knowledge gathering. Young people today are aware of these problems, but this by itself does not mean they are capable of reflective moral action.

Twenty years ago many predicted a decline in the influence of religion in the UK, assuming there would come a time when religious education would have little or no relevance in secular schools. Global events during the first decade of the twenty-first century have shown this to have been a false assumption (see for example World Bank, 2006). With increasing globalization of faith and conflict of values has come a realization that the place of religion in the public sphere has to be taken seriously. In this chapter I argue that there is a need to form a pedagogy for religious education which honours the authenticity of faith for the believer, takes its position in human experience and daily life seriously as well as offering a means by which those with a secular world view can access the deep significance of religious faith for a believer.

The Impact of Globalization on Religious Education

During the first decade of the twenty-first century the religious landscape of the UK has changed. There has been a continuing secularization, with the population as a whole accepting less and less influence from religious authorities. Despite this, there remains the continued structural influence of the Anglican Church in our constitutional arrangements. This continuing influence is discussed now in a new social context where the depth and strength of those practising non-Christian faiths is coming into play. We are for sure a plural democracy in the UK; we have a reasonably good track record over the last 150 years of adapting provision so that our children may have the best education and social environment. How are these new challenges going to move us forward?

For many years during the post-war rise of secularism we have thought that the divide between public life and personal life in terms of religious influence was clear; however, the globalization of Islam in particular has challenged this assumption. There is a realization in government and beyond that in order to work for the cohesion of the whole nation the impact of religion upon public life through explicit exemplification of religious belief must be taken into account. (see for example Ofsted 2010). The same is happening across Europe, but in the UK specifically, religious education was always concerned with promoting the control of the state and of the established church over religious practice (see for example Cox, 1983, especially Chapter 1). Where the influence of religion in society was declining, religious education could well be considered a Cinderella subject on the curriculum; however, in the present climate religious education is able to help schools determine their own values and recognize the importance of personal faith and world vision in the lives of its students and their families. The question is whether religious education will be able to rise to this challenge, to loose itself from the influence of the churches and see itself in educational terms and relevance alone (see, for example, Maylor, 2007). Education has been seen for a while to be a kind of "product" to be consumed by "learners", monitored by "stakeholders" and communicated like any other product by "teachers" expert in the delivery of "teaching and learning packages", with head teachers marketing the particular "product" on sale in their particular school. In light of present crises, perhaps we can now revert to what is needed for the well-being of human society and place young people and their families together with schools and educators as partners in a project of national significance.

In the most simplistic way it could be said that specific religions or discrete faith systems have a dual purpose: to give explanations regarding the origin of all things, and to offer a system of determining what really matters. Religious faith in a secular world must be seen as one possible way of giving meaning to the answers to these questions. What is beyond doubt now is that these questions themselves are important and worthy of consideration in the school curriculum. Furthermore it can be argued that questions relating to what really matters about how we should live, or what formed the universe, or whether men and women are equal or whether it is right or wrong to kill, have become central to education. Understanding this is critical. In a world that has had to face up to the fact that education properly engages with both the inner and outer world of children and young people's lives, we can see that in plural societies there can be no one absolute, certain knowledge about any of these things. Understanding and inquiry become instead the central tools of the educator and specifically of the religious educator, who is working in the territory where there is often disagreement about these key questions of life.

A purely knowledge based pedagogy, therefore, requiring students to learn about religious practices, is out of the question for RE. Disagreement within religions may make any piece of information soon outdated or even completely inaccurate, and there is another problem: knowledge takes us into the philosophical domain of epistemology and ontology. In matters of importance between religions it is unlikely that there can ever be complete agreement about facts, for example about the origin of things or of what really matters, so we need something else around which to form our pedagogy.

Globalization's immense impact upon religious education continues as we move further into the twenty-first century. With increased migration, it is important to bring together communities with different belief systems so that they share an identity as a nation. Knowing about each other will be a necessary part of that but it will not be sufficient. Without also crafting understanding and indeed a depth of interest in the well-being of the other who is different from me, knowledge can lead to intolerance and misunderstanding. The proposal in this chapter is that the way forward with this will be some kind of inquiry methodology. That inquiry, particularly when engaged in with others in community, brings the possibility of weaving together our inner meaning-making with our action in the world. The next section of this chapter discusses inquiry pedagogy and moves to a proposal from which to develop the penultimate section of this chapter at some length.

I suggest here that we need a critical shift in our foundations of religious education, a shift similar to that which has happened recently in maths and science. Here it is seen that the key processes of mathematical and scientific inquiry are the things that need to be communicated and that these skills and aptitudes are at the heart of what is needed to both understand the subject and be enthused by it.

In the rest of this chapter I will explore the nature of inquiry and suggest a sketch of what it could look like in religious education.

What Do We Mean by Inquiry?

Here I seek to give an account of the nature of inquiry which will allow us to shine light upon why this is important for religious education in a plural democracy. Inquiry seems to be a possible form of human living that we need in order to progress and develop full adult potential. Children thrive on this relentless exploration: it seems to be the way they find out information and again and again find and reshape meaning in their fast-changing lives. My working hypothesis here is that inquiry has as its aim the resolution of a problem or question. It also affects the way people behave or relate to others in their lives. The kinds of questions which are open for inquiry could be scientific questions or moral questions or questions about the nature of something, or even a question about how we answer questions themselves. Inquiry is an important process for us to be able to undertake well wherever there is some uncertainty or disagreement about the facts of the matter. It also compels us to move into the new and uncertain, to adventure and explore.

When we are thinking about investigating especially puzzling questions, we will probably be clear at the beginning whether we expect to reach one final answer. Take murder for example. Imagine you are discussing with your friends whether it could ever be right to murder. Someone might start out with the fixed view that it is always wrong. Whether they know it or not they are holding to a theory – a moral theory – that wants to say that somewhere there is a true answer to this matter. Now imagine the conversation develops. You give the example of a woman who is alone in the house with her small children. Someone comes in and tries to harm one of the children. Could it ever be right for her to attack and kill the intruder?

This is an example where it may not be exactly clear whether the action is right or not. Taking a morally absolute line can possibly be unhelpful when looking at these kinds of problems. A branch of philosophy where there are people who have worked on trying to understand these kinds of moral and other ambiguities is known as pragmatism. For philosophers such as Charles Sanders Peirce, William James, John Dewey, and others, inquiry is the key way we are going to be able to reach any understanding of such questions which inevitably have ambiguity about them. Peirce was particularly interested in the links between knowledge and inquiry, William James had a particular interest in how we change our minds on different matters, and Dewey was greatly concerned about the relationship between inquiry and democracy and how these things relate to education (see especially Dewey, 1916).

Inquiry seems to have a double edge. There is the matter we have just discussed about how it can help us resolve or make progress in our understanding of difficult questions. This is how it relates to the branches of philosophy we know as epistemology and ethics – how we know things at all and how we know things in the area of morality.

Clearly in a plural democracy giving space in schools for young people to develop their capacity to investigate moral questions is of prime importance. Matthew Lipman, who developed the Philosophy for Children programme in the 1960s[1], suggested that introducing children to the tools and procedures of ethical inquiry is in effect, to prepare them to engage in reasoned moral practice (Lipman, 1988: 79). In a time where there is moral uncertainty surely there could be little more important a task. In these ways inquiry can help us develop our capacity to make informed moral judgements – ones they have reflected on. In a society where there is a plurality of faith, developing the capacity for inquiry through our educational systems will be essential where there are different views about why things are as they are in the universe, about what things are important and about how we should live. So when we support the application of tools of inquiry to such questions, about what is important and what principles we should use to guide our lives, we are genuinely helping young people begin to engage in an inquiry into faith and help them begin to form considered judgements about faith. Perhaps nothing is more important in a world where faith plays such a part in regional conflicts as well as bringing harmony between peoples.

Communities of Inquiry

Lipman went on (2003) to propose that when we work together in a community of inquiry we multiply the effort; our shared inquiry will have more creative possibility than if we simply work alone. There is a close connection with inquiry in community and sound reasoning. Sometimes we can make mistakes in our reasoning. Working together with others in communities of inquiry brings more opportunity for developing the checks and balances necessary so that we can be open to others pointing out our mistakes. Perhaps it does not always follow that there will be a particular outcome from a particular situation. Another member of the class community can point this out by giving an example or counter example. How much more powerful for the class if this comes from another member of the group and not just the teacher and how much more likely is a young person to change their mind influenced by the critical but caring reasoning of their peers in a carefully facilitated community of inquiry.

Reasoning includes such things as defining, giving examples and counter examples, comparing, contrasting and distinguishing between things. Being able to identify and suggest valid inferences as well as thinking hypothetically (what if . . .?) are all important things to be able to do in our shared inquiries. In a community of inquiry the role of the teacher changes dramatically to become a facilitator of the young people's conversation. No longer does the teacher hold the knowledge or the answer to the closed question. The teacher's role becomes one to support the young people's inquiry by for example encouraging *them* to give examples and counter examples, checking back with the group that there are no false assumptions being made, and supporting their capacity to distinguish and differentiate.

From this we find there comes another impact on the students who engage in classroom communities of inquiry. It is not just that they can make better objective assessments or judgements of situations which are being investigated in the community, but we also find that the way students relate to each other in the class changes. Further, the way that the students consider themselves and their ideas about important matters also changes. They become more serious and more able to engage deeply with the significance of the issues and questions. In other words the impact of inquiry on those who share in it is personal. This impact is noticeable and continuing. In this way communities of inquiry begin to develop a character of their own and the participants change. It becomes more possible for them to live out the results of the explorations which have taken place.

> Everyone has their own say and listens and thinks more because other people are saying what they think. You can disagree and say why you think their reasons are not strong ones. It helps me to develop my own ideas and beliefs about the world. (Nathan, 14, quoted in Hannam and Echeverria, 2009)

In this way we find that inquiry can impact on the understanding of a particular problem or question explored and that this leads further to a personal impact on the way people live their life. It will be argued here that this double effect makes it useful for forming educational theory for religious education in a plural democracy, which takes the significance of difference seriously. This will be developed further in the next section of this chapter.

Gilbert Ryle (1980) suggests that thinking is a very particular kind of activity which enables us to relate our inner selves to the world. Inquiry is for sure a kind of thinking. The kinds of skills that are developed when we are inquiring or thinking *together* in communities of inquiry are those such as explanation, formulation, hypothesis-making, judgement, evidence-giving. These things together with the reasoning skills mentioned above we would regard as higher order thinking skills.

In a world which is increasingly uncertain, developing genuine opportunities for shared inquiry will be essential. At a time when the religious complexity of a society is leading towards potential fragmentation and where divisions can lead to intolerance, funding educationally sound processes for working creatively with difference will be of the utmost importance.

The proposal to be developed in the rest of this chapter is that forming our religious education classrooms into communities of collaborative, caring yet critical inquiry will be helpful when we are exploring matters relating to the origin and nature of things and to determining what is important – the essential characteristics of religions. Therefore inquiry can support reflection on the ways we should live our lives and transform the actual way we live in the light of these inquiries. Here we can offer a genuine opportunity to value difference, to give emphasis on the relationship between dialogue and inquiry and build a view on how this can work to support understanding of difference in a general context of life in a plural democracy.

The contribution of the pedagogical proposal of Philosophy for Children as developed originally by Lipman (1998, 2003) and Sharp and Splitter (1995) with their proposal of forming our classrooms into communities of philosophical inquiry will be considered. This will include a critical discussion of the distinctive character of philosophical inquiry and any other inquiry.

Why Is Inquiry Significant at This Time for Religious Education?

When we are planning to develop our classrooms into communities of inquiry in RE, we are going to support the students in their capability to raise and formulate significant and puzzling questions about matters which are in the field of concern for religion and faith. We are going to facilitate their inquiries by developing their capacity for higher order thinking through encouraging good reasoning such as giving examples and counter examples, recognizing false assumptions. A further aspect of inquiry which comes from the capacity to formulate questions is the development of the ability to recognise and work with concepts. Concepts are kinds of big ideas that attempt to encapsulate things that are important for us. The concepts of love, hope, freedom, belonging, God, belief, friendship, and heaven will all come up in the RE classroom.

Inquiry is not a new concept in religious education. Clive Erricker and those working with him in Hampshire developed a conceptual inquiry approach to religious education through the agreed syllabus *Living Difference* published in 2004 (see also Erricker, 2005). This approach is in contrast with more epistemological approaches to RE such as the critical realism of Andrew Wright (e.g. 2001, 2006, 2007) or the more anthropological proposal of the interpretive approach of Robert Jackson (e.g. 1997, 2004). The conceptual inquiry approach to RE divides concepts into three broad categories. The first, called Type A concepts, are those which are general to all human experience such as friendship and love. Type B concepts are those which are used by all or some religions; they are clearly religious concepts but not necessarily specific and particular to only one religion. Such concepts would include God, worship, prayer, and faith. There is a further kind of concept (Type C) which is specific to particular religions: Umma, Sangha, atonement, the body of Christ and incarnation would fit into this group of concepts.

Such a categorization of concepts can be very helpful when we are planning to develop an inquiry led programme in RE where we are working to develop young people's capacity to work with concepts. But concepts alone, although important, are not the only thing necessary in inquiry in the religious education classroom. We also need to develop the capacities of inquiry and reasoning. This is where we have a great deal to learn from the work of Matthew Lipman and others in the pedagogical proposal of the community of philosophical inquiry, often known as Philosophy for Children (P4C).

Plurality of faith has always been with us in the UK; to suggest otherwise would be inaccurate. Indeed Hannah Arendt tells us that plurality is the nature of human action (Arendt, 1998: 7). Hence when we work in religious education we should not be surprised to be working with a plurality of faiths and I would want to argue that religious faith is indeed a form of human action in the way Arendt conceives. What has changed in the UK in the past 30 years is the increasing likelihood of a multiplicity of faith being represented in our classrooms in most schools and the consequences or implications for the advancement of community cohesion in our national, local and school communities. In the 1970s the first agreed syllabuses were being written to take account of multicultural approaches to RE. Since this time all agreed syllabuses for religious education have treated religion as if it were something objective to be studied, as if with some kind of religious knowledge through learning about religion we would somehow come to understand each other better. Clearly this is not necessarily so.

As Biesta (2006: 102) suggests, there is a key consequence of the increasing multiplicity of faith in our schools. This is that we must now question whether we can think objectively any more about plurality. Although we can accept that we live in a plural world, can we speak at all in a neutral way about this plurality? If we accept that we now live in a plural democracy and that remaining neutral in regard to these social changes is impossible, then determining ways of working with this plurality in terms of religion in our school classrooms becomes even more sensitive. The subject of this curricular subject *is* distinct from other disciplines. RE can for sure no longer be about knowledge transmission, or even primarily about concept formation, but is much more related to processes which help develop the understanding of difference.

Diversity is a key concept talked about in education (see Maylor, 2007 and Ofsted, 2008 for legislation and guidance regarding equality and diversity). It is suggested that acknowledging diversity is a way we can work towards equality of opportunity. However, it is still possible that by simply acknowledging diversity we are leading to a kind of sorting exercise with ever more categories, none sufficient to explain the reality of our world. All such categorization leads to the suggestion that our diversity in a plural world can be explained in terms of mere cultural or conceptual categories. This is unsatisfactory as it masks the significance that differences have for people of faith. It leads to an epistemological understanding of plurality which divides.

By viewing plurality, as Arendt does, as an essential part of human existence, we begin to turn the concern round. We begin to appreciate that the most significant questions arising for religious education from the fact of plurality of belief are essentially questions of existence rather than of knowledge. This way we can see the heart of religious education in existential terms rather ones of knowledge transmission. We can begin to conceive of a place for a kind of existential inquiry as the first principle of religious education in plural communities, rather than principles relating to learning or knowledge.

A conversation with some of the concerns of Dewey, one of our key pragmatist philosophers, in one of his key works – *On Certainty* – (1960) - becomes most pertinent at this point. Dewey asks us to consider whether inquiry can itself become a vehicle for understanding and attaining some kind of knowledge and whether even there is another way of knowing in the face of plurality and uncertainty. He invites us to consider whether there is a way of knowing that does not put us into the position of making judgements about this or that, a way of knowing that involves us standing in a different relationship with the reality we are judging. Dewey suggests that this other way of knowing involves us being inside the universe we are part of and so the process of knowing becomes an engagement with the interconnectedness of things rather than something cognitive and separate from existence.

Following on from this and linking with the thinking of Hannah Arendt (1998) we can realize that the root of our work in RE is a moral one and with the pedagogical process of inquiry we can begin to state this clearly.

Focussing on transforming our classrooms into communities of inquiry, and in particular communities of philosophical inquiry into questions of religious significance, will help us resolve the conundrum for religious education, that it can no longer be primarily be about transmission of knowledge about facts about religions and yet understanding some of these things will be important. If we are truly moving away from an epistemological basis of the subject to a moral justification of the subject, we need to examine something else altogether. The proposal for the shared action of philosophical inquiry will form this basis.

The Community of Philosophical Inquiry in Religious Education

> In a philosophical inquiry you get to hear other people's points of view. There are lots of voices in the world, and in an inquiry you get to hear some of them. I have learned to appreciate that people can think differently from me. Sometimes I might change my mind about an idea or think about something in a way I had not thought of before. (Becky, 14, quoted in Hannam and Echeverria, 2009)

Why "philosophical inquiry" and not "religious inquiry" in religious education?

I want to suggest that religious inquiry is the business of people who have consciously decided to investigate the religious way of life as a commitment for themselves. In a plural society which is predominantly secular I suggest this is not justifiable as a methodology in religious education in secular schools. Rather we need to give the tools of philosophical inquiry which will facilitate the investigation and understanding of the great questions before us regarding the origin of things and what is important for our lives. This offers a frame where there can be the shared examination in our classroom communities of various life stances – religious and otherwise – the central theme of investigation remaining constant. Since the time of Socrates, Plato, and Aristotle the tools of philosophical inquiry have served us well and I suggest can continue to do so. These tools can enable us to access the depths of human experience and at the same time allow us to engage with more clarity in matters of shared subjective concern.

The "community of philosophical inquiry" in the form of "philosophy for children" (P4C) was conceived and developed by Matthew Lipman in the 1960s and developed further at the Institute for the Advancement of Philosophy for Children (IAPC). It is a pedagogical proposal – a pedagogical model – and is recognized worldwide within a framework of many different programmes for teaching thinking skills. Philosophy for children, however, is more than just a thinking-skills programme; it also makes a proposal about the kind of society that is desirable and about the kind of people we should be forming through the educational system, based on values associated with the concept of democracy.

The structure of a session in a community of philosophical inquiry

There are several steps that are typical of what happens in a classical community of philosophical inquiry:

1. A stimulus is offered to the students. It should be something of interest to them, which raises problems and has the potential to evoke philosophical question.
2. Questions are developed.
3. A question is chosen as the heart of the dialogue in the community.
4. There is engagement in dialogue and philosophical exploration, carefully facilitated by the teacher/facilitator, of the chosen question. Here hypotheses will be formed and tested, concepts clarified and assumptions aired.
5. There will be some kind of closure to the session.
6. The session will be evaluated.\xnl\

Dialogical inquiry in our classroom communities in religious education, where there can be conflict over truth claims, has an especially valuable part to play in helping young people develop their own sense of identity and belonging. Through helping them to work out with their peers, their values and beliefs about questions relating to the origin of things and what things really matter to them; philosophical inquiry in religious education facilitates a growing appreciation of belief and culture in the world today. The teacher becomes the facilitator of their conversation, deepening the investigation through the use of follow up questions.

The kind of question that could arise in a philosophical inquiry in a religious education lesson could be "Are people more important than animals?" This is a point upon which different religious traditions do not exactly agree. A key part of this question is the phrase "more important than". The community working with this question would need to have some criteria for making judgements about what would count as more important.

How could we possibly decide this? What would it depend upon? Before working with the question, and while doing so, we begin to build criteria, or a list of qualifying statements that would inform the judgement. For example, such a list of criteria could include "better than", "more useful than" and so on until the group felt that there were sufficient to build understanding for everyone in that community. The all-encompassing nature of a curriculum developed around philosophical inquiry will lend itself to the further development of teacher understanding. Soon, teachers will be able to build significant philosophical meaning into lessons.

There are some key concepts in these questions as well, for example the concept of "human being". Here we can see that through a process of inquiry young people become more expert at conceptual clarification. Indeed we can say that philosophical inquiry as applied to religious education would facilitate this conceptual clarification – of all types of concepts as differentiated by the work of the Hampshire agreed syllabus.

Philosophical inquiry in religious education is:

- a process of developing philosophical conceptualization.
- a process advancing skills of logical, hypothetical and inferential reasoning. ("Does it always follow that . . . ?" "What if . . . ?" "Could you give an example . . . ?" "If . . . is true then what follows?"
- It will advance the development of a moral imagination by helping young people to become more open to taking responsibility for their own thinking and subsequent action.
- An opportunity for young people to be in the position to examine their ideas in a context of their own *and* in relation to a religious context, alongside the ideas of others.
- An opportunity to determine means of making informed philosophical judgements about matters of religious significance.

Young people who have had the opportunity to experience philosophical inquiry over a period of time can work confidently with ambiguity and uncertainty. Philosophy for children as developed by Lipman was underpinned by a desire to advance what can be understood as being "good reasoning". This is not just logical reasoning but can also be exemplified by collaborative reasoning and shared thinking. It is not simply being able to reason, or to be rational; rather reasonableness combined with sound thinking and clear conceptualization forms people who are able to make strong ethical decisions and to live well.

Working with philosophical concepts is something that we do in religious education frequently. A community of inquiry is philosophical when the teacher/facilitator encourages students to take the inquiry deeper into the ideas raised. The teacher must be able to recognize a philosophical idea or concept when it comes up. Religious education teachers often have a good understanding here. Philosophical concepts relevant to religious education include justice, love, responsibility, freedom, friendship, hope, God and what it means to be human. However, this way of working will also give opportunity for exploration of more specific religious concepts such as Umma, Sangha or the Body of Christ, enabling the formation of subtle and delicate understanding. When we then begin to look at this in relation to my actions as a result of another inquiry into, say, "'community", we can see how philosophical exploration of matters of religious could begin to inform action a life the school, the local and national communities.

Conclusion: Implications for an Inquiry Based Pedagogy

The surest way to guarantee the best outcomes in the classroom with philosophical inquiry is to ensure that the facilitator who will work with the young people in this new way is suitably prepared. Most aspects of regular teacher training in British universities at this time do not fully prepare new teachers to work with young people in this more informal way. Philosophical inquiry is not a conventional educational approach that requires the teacher to follow an outline plan or a programme published in an established syllabus or government curriculum document. Working effectively with the community of philosophical inquiry is a much more complex project. It entails the teacher being exposed to the ambiguities of religions and their responses to life's great questions. Teachers in training need to be able to appreciate the contribution of education to the well being of humanity rather than simply being deliverers of a product. This is going to require a transformation of our teacher training institutions also into communities of inquiry. We can start by placing a philosophical consideration of education at the heart of teacher training and beginning our work from there.

All in all the proposal here has been that for a religious education capable of responding to the key questions facing us regarding the place of religion in civic society and the response which education needs to make in the light of this, we need to move to an inquiry pedagogy in our classrooms. If we can do this we may just be able to develop sufficient moral and religious imagination to allow religion to take the place in human society it both desires and deserves. This is to help us on our journey as human beings together as we explore what kind of creatures we are and what kind of shared world we should like to form for ourselves on our planet – in other words, to explore with due seriousness the questions of the nature of the origin of things and which things are really important to our survival.

Note

1 The 'community of philosophical inquiry' in the form of 'philosophy for children' (P4C) was conceived and developed by Matthew Lipman in the 1960s and developed further at the Institute for the Advancement of Philosophy for Children (IAPC). It is a pedagogical proposal – a pedagogical model – and is recognized worldwide within a framework of many different programmes for teaching thinking skills. Philosophy for children, however, is more than just a thinking-skills programme; it also makes a proposal about the kind of society that is desirable and about the kind of people we should be forming through the educational system, based on values associated with the concept of democracy. When Matthew Lipman was Professor of Philosophy at Columbia University, New York, in the 1960s, he realized that young people were frequently and often justifiably uncomfortable with some of the features of the society in which they were living. He found some of their concerns very reasonable but he also realized that they lacked the necessary skills to construct sound arguments to fight for what they thought was right. Out of these concerns was borne the P4C programme now existing on over 60 countries worldwide.

References

Arendt, H. 1998. *The Human Condition.* 2nd ed. London. University of Chicago Press.

Biesta, G.J.J. 2006. *Beyond Learning: Democratic Education for a Human Future.* Boulder, CO. Paradigm.

Biesta, G.J.J., and Burbules, N.C. 2003. *Pragmatism and Educational Research.* Oxford. Rowman and Littlefield.

Cox, E. 1983. *Problems and Possibilities for Religious Education.* London. Hodder and Stoughton.

Dewey, J. 1916. *Democracy and Education: An Introduction to the Philosophy of Education.* New York. Free Press.

Dewey, J. 1960. O*n Certainty: A Study of the Relation of Knowledge and Action.* Capricorn Books.

Erricker, C. 2005. 'Bike riding for beginners: living difference and a methodology for teaching and learning in RE', *World Religions and Education . . . yearbook.* Cambridge. Hobsons.

Fesmire, S. 2003. *John Dewey and Moral Imagination: Pragmatism in Ethics.* Bloomington. Indiana University Press.

Hannam, P., and Echeverria, E. 2009. *Philosophy with Teenagers: Nurturing a Moral Imagination for the 21st Century*. London. Continuum.

Jackson, R. 1997. *Religious Education: An Interpretive Approach.* London. Hodder and Stoughton.

Jackson, R. 2004. *Rethinking Religious Education and Plurality: Issues in Diversity and Pedagogy.* London. RoutledgeFalmer.

Lipman, M. 1988. *Philosophy Goes to School.* Philadelphia. Temple University Press.

Lipman, M. 2003. *Thinking in Education.* 2nd ed. Cambridge. Cambridge University Press.
Maylor, U., et al. 2007. *Diversity and Citizenship in the Curriculum: Research Review*. Nottingham. DfES.
Ofsted. 2008. Race Equality Scheme
Ofsted. 2010. *Inspecting Maintained Schools' Duty to Promote Community Cohesion: Guidance for Inspectors.* Manchester. Ofsted.
Ryle, G. 1979. *On Thinking.* Oxford. Blackwell.
Sharp, A.M., and Splitter, L.J. 1995. *Teaching for Better Thinking.* Melbourne, Vic. ACER.
World Bank. 2006. *World Development Report 2007: Development and the Next Generation.* Washington, DC. World Bank.
Wright, A. 2001. 'Dancing in the Fire: A Deconstruction of Clive Erricker's Postmodern Spiritual Pedagogy', *Religious Education,* 96(1): 120–135.
Wright, A. 2007. *Critical Religious Education, Multiculturalism and the Pursuit of Truth*. Cardiff. University of Wales Press.
Wright, A. 2006. 'Critical Realism as a Tool for the Interpretation of Cultural Diversity in Liberal Religious Education', *International Handbook of the Religious, Moral and Spiritual Dimensions of Education* (eds M. de Souza et al.). London. Springer. Vol. 1: 333–347.

Chapter Eight

Creativity and Reflection in Religious Education: Refreshes the Parts Other Approaches Can't Reach

Emma McVittie

In this chapter I will look at how RE can be used as a vehicle to explore creativity and reflection. I wanted to engage students of primary initial teacher education (ITE) to think about RE in a different way and encourage them to take these ideas forward into a primary school setting. It is based around a case study of the RE specialist theme within my institution.

The poem that follows has remained with me since I was 16 and is the foundation of my philosophy of primary teaching.

He Always

He always wanted to explain things
But no-one cared
So he drew.
Sometimes he would draw and it wasn't anything
He wanted to carve it in stone
Or write it in the sky,
He would lie out on the grass
And look up at the sky
And it would be only the sky
and the things inside him that needed saying.
And it was after that,
He drew the picture.
It was a beautiful picture
He kept it under his pillow
And would let no one see it,
And he would look at it every night
And think about it.
And when it was dark

And his eyes were closed
He could still see it
And it was all of him
And he loved it.
When he started school he brought it with him
Not to show anyone but just to have it with him
Like a friend.
It was funny about school
He sat in a square brown desk
Like all the other square brown desks
And he thought it should be red.
And his room was a square brown room
Like all the other rooms
And it was tight and close
And stiff.
He hated to hold the pencil and chalk
With his arms stiff and his feet flat on the floor
Stiff
With the teacher watching
And watching.
The teacher came and smiled at him
She told him to wear a tie
Like all the other boys
He said he didn't like them
And she said it didn't matter.
After that they drew
And he drew all yellow
And it was the way he felt about the morning
And it was beautiful.
The teacher came and smiled at him
"What's this?" she said
"Why don't you draw something like Ken's drawing?"
"Isn't that beautiful?"
After that his mother bought him a tie
And he always drew airplanes and rocket ships
Like everyone else
And he threw the old picture away.
And when he lay out alone and looked out at the sky
It was big and blue and all of everything
But he wasn't anymore

He was square and brown inside
And his hands were stiff
And he was like everyone else
And the things inside him that needed saying
Didn't need it anymore
It had stopped pushing
It was crushed
Stiff
Like everything else.

Anonymous

Do we stop using our imagination or stop being creative after the age of four? The early years and foundation stage framework talks about the importance of learning through play and exploration while emphasizing the importance of creative connections and states that "it is difficult for children to make creative connections in learning while making a Diwali card like everyone else" (QCDA, 2007). Children don't suddenly stop "playing" when they learn to read and write; neither does it become acceptable for everyone to express themselves in identical ways. I have worked in a variety of educational settings from residential special to mainstream rural schools and the one thing that all these children have in common, regardless of their difficulties, is the need to be heard and communicate their responses. For those children who find it difficult to do this, we often provide alternatives such as a sensory room, picture exchange system or using the senses. However, this is generally only available for those whose needs are obvious and diagnosed. What happens to those children who sit at the back of the class and put their hand up just as you're asking another child the answer, those who labour to produce accepted writing and those who just feel so sure they will fail that they don't even try? Maybe keeping their options open through a creative approach is the answer – certainly not to all our problems, but at least it may give those children a chance to reach their potential. Personally if a child handed me something "all yellow" and said it was the way they felt about the morning, I'd be delighted!

There are two clear concepts related to this approach. One is associated with thinking and learning creatively, the second is concerned with being creative, demonstrating learning in a creative way. Children (and adults) need to learn how to think in a creative manner in order to achieve their full potential whether in education or business. Innovative and independent thinkers are needed in all walks of life; this may mean changing their mind-set completely and defining what creativity isn't rather than what it is.

> Creativity is not unique to the arts, but fundamental to advances in Science, Maths, and technology. This is because creativity is a form of thinking, a mode of operating that isn't bound by subject, and can be demonstrated in any aspect of life. (Howlett, 2009)

Creativity isn't just about the arts, it isn't an isolated activity, and it isn't just "nice in theory"; it's an ability, an attitude, and a process. Creativity is also subjective; a single definition cannot cover the extent of creative thinking and what that means to an individual. According to the National Curriculum (1999), thinking creatively involves asking "why?", "how?" and "what if?", and these are the same questions we are encouraging children to ask in RE lessons, using curiosity to gain a better understanding of their own lives and the people around them.

Religious education is perfectly placed to integrate both concepts as the skills involved in the attainment targets (AT1 and AT2) for RE are key in developing creative thinking and encouraging personal response:

> It includes the skills of interpretation, analysis and explanation. It develops pupils' skills of application, interpretation and evaluation of what they learn about religion . . . and communicating their responses. (QCA, 2004: 34)

It is a subject which involves not only knowledge, skills and understanding but where positive attitudes to learning are developed which are not dependent upon academic prowess. This enables all children to participate at their own level of understanding and experience and opens the door to a creative approach to learning. Integral to this is reflection, which is embedded in RE and forms one of its foundation stones. The key outcome of reflection is judged to be learning, the extent of which is largely dependent on cognitive and affective responses. These responses vary and are supplemented depending on the purpose. We learn when we do something with information, when we take it apart and reorganize it, yet too often children just regurgitate information in the same form as it was given. Dewey (1938) stated that in order for effective learning to take place, the conditions must engage the student with content in an intensely personal way. Rogers (1969) agrees and adds that "the subject matter must have relevance to result in significant learning" (Cited in Moon, 2006). RE has all the elements needed to enable reflection to take place and have a significant impact on learning through the use of children's experiences and responses to the world around them alongside consideration of the fundamental questions in life. The agreed syllabus *Living Difference* attempts to encompass current approaches by allowing children to journey through concepts through skills of inquiry rather than just accumulating content:

- **Inquire** into the concept. They explore it and unpack the meaning of it.
- **Contextualise** the concept within the expression of faith: its beliefs, values, practices.
- **Evaluate** by appreciating why people do what they do or say what they say (evaluate from within) and by weighing up the issues and implications that are raised (evaluate from without) and articulating their opinions about the ways in which the concept is expressed.
- **Communicate** their own personal responses to their experiences of the concept in focus.
- **Apply** their own responses to the concept to different situations and circumstances in their own and others' lives.

(Erricker and Costambeys, 2005)

This cycle of learning demonstrates the potential of RE to be a creative and reflective subject not only in its pedagogical approach but in the way children express their responses and ideas in the classroom.

The link between Reflection and Creativity: Creative Responses to Reflections

The case study

RE generally has minimal input into primary initial teacher training and there is a lack of exposure to good practice in the school-based element of the programme. "This is an historic shortcoming which has created a cycle of under-performance" (REC, 2007). From the prespective of an individual institution, the hours for RE have been reduced over the years and this in turn means the subject is viewed as being of reduced importance. Although RE is gaining momentum within certain circles, it is losing its hold in others. In response to this I wanted to generate interest and excitement about RE within ITE. Too often students are expected (and sometimes expect) to regurgitate information presented. The approach I have used allows freedom and space to learn. However the students did find this hard to cope with in the beginning: they wanted structure and to be told how to do things. After all, this is what the majority of education promotes and it is difficult to break this mould of there always being a right and a wrong answer. Students would constantly ask "Is this right?" when it is not always the product that is of importance but the process itself. As we progressed, they felt more able to contribute their thoughts and feelings and to express them in a variety of ways without feeling under pressure to get the "right" answer. They began to realize that it was their personal journey and interpretation of experience that mattered.

The module aims to develop students' understanding of the links between religious education and creativity in relation to global and environmental perspectives. The learning objectives were designed to allow students the space to think about innovative ways to teach RE in relation to their personal and professional experiences so far.

Students will:

i Be able to **evaluate** the appropriateness of creative approaches when teaching religious education in the primary classroom.

ii Be able to **investigate** the opportunities for encouraging awe and wonder within the primary curriculum and its relationship to spirituality.

iii Be able to **reflect** upon personal and professional experiences of religious education and evaluate their influence with reference to a range of sources.

iv Be able to **explore** concepts and principles underpinning the responses from faith traditions to issues of global concern.

An essential part of the module was reflection and this was supported throughout by reference to a teaching model (Fig. 8-1) and the use of reflective journals. The model is not cyclical and does not follow a consecutive pattern but it is hierarchical, based on the depth of reflection from basic reflection to reflexive learning (Parahoo, 1997). The students were guided through each level during the module:

- Recall description
- Analytical reflection
- Contextual reflection
- Critical reflection
- Active reflection (reflexive learning)

The rational is that the person, along with the event or experience, will jump to the particular type of reflection that is appropriate for that situation and that time. They may then move to the next level to deepen their learning and understanding or may choose to go straight to active reflection. It is possible to go from any of the levels straight to active reflection, missing out the deeper reflective stages. These are the stages we, as educators, need to develop; we

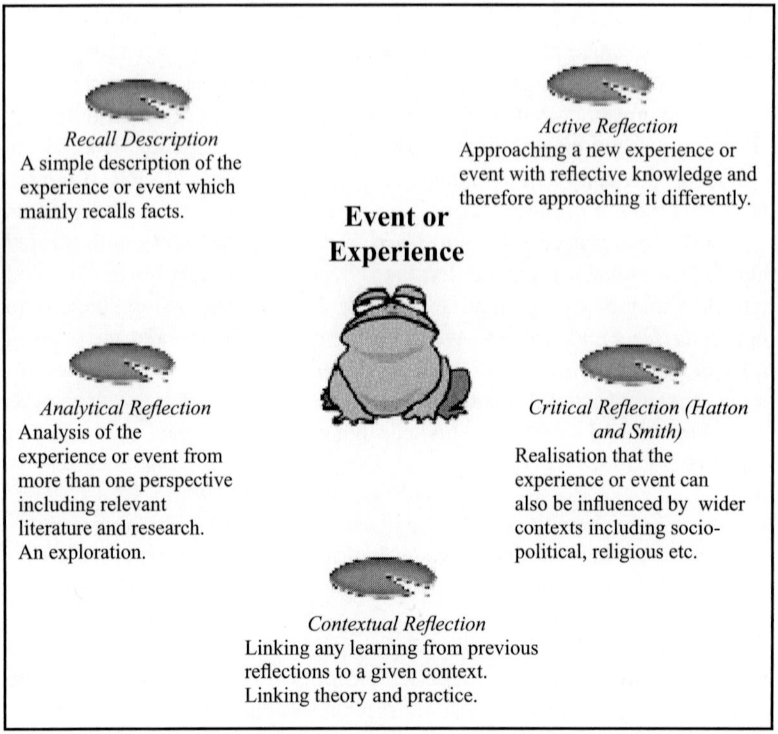

Fig. 8-1

need to model the skills required for students to do this. This process is often subconscious but, by using this model within teaching, greater attention is drawn to these actions and students can be provided with tools to enable them to consciously deepen their learning, including some form of dialogue. External and internal forms of dialogue are prominent within religious education due to discussion, the questioning, inquiring nature of the subject and the challenging issues that are raised. Bakhtin (1981) comments on the internal and external forms of this dialogue. I propose that there are two aspects of internal dialogue. The *primary, internal* aspect of dialogue can only be theorized about due to its intrinsic quality and personal dimension as it is a spontaneous discourse that is only known to the individual. However, the *secondary* aspect involves the dialogue being recognized and formalized through reflection and the discourse begins to take place in a verbal or written manner. Within this context, this occurred through reflective journals.

This model was created last year in response to growing frustration about the use of reflection in higher education within education courses.

When this theoretical classification was considered in relation to existing practice, it became clear that there was no collective understanding of the process or of how to engage students with reflection for learning. This and the heightening importance of individualized learning promoted in higher education institutions and the government's creativity agenda, has led me to develop this approach to encourage true engagement with RE. If we are increasing the use of independent learning then it is important that students know how to approach tasks and learn from them effectively with limited face to face contact. I believe that the reflective process holds the key and will aid students' transformative learning. Rather than asking students to remember facts and theories, we want them to challenge and question in order to further their own knowledge. Learning is an important element of higher education and although it can happen unconsciously, it also needs to be directed and informed. This learning may be deepened by the use of reflection:

> Reflection can never be objectified or discerned as an isolated method or technique, supporting an individual's growth of knowledge. Instead reflection is a lived process, involving human beings in their entirety. (Ekebergh, 2007)

I see reflective learning as a process with a variety of pathways depending on the level of reflection. Reflection does not have a definition. The theories are fluid and are not fact: to truly understand reflection, you need to experience it and be inside it. Some don't see the value of recording reflection as they feel that they can reflect without writing it down. This is true; writing is only a further representation of reflection and can often represent some form of dialogue. "In making a representation of personal reflection, we shape and model the content of our reflection in different ways and learn also from the process itself" (Moon, 2004: 80).

Reflective learning is an amalgamation of processes which can be both intentional and incidental. Reflective learning may change our thinking or reinforce a concept, but the learning is not always immediate and may be moulded over time. This happens because reflection is a process. Sometimes there is an input, sometimes not, but there may be an outcome irrespective of this. Description has a role in reflection but it needs to be focussed to enable it to be developed. Reflection isn't used to define *all* thinking. Reflection and critical thinking can overlap: reflection is more about exploration and walking around things, whereas critical thinking involves the development of a judgement; however, they have characteristics in common. We also reflect on complex processes; the complexity depends on your perspective. When you enter Hatton and Smith's (1995) critical reflection you will be aware of varying perspectives which will increase the complexity and change your perceptions of the event. Inevitably this will increase the emotion, which is in all learning though we pay it more attention in reflection. You can only reflect within your own range of perception; you need to draw on others' opinions and experiences of the same event to achieve deep reflection and possibly critical thinking. It is evident that there is a unique vocabulary associated with reflection. For example, reflective learning and reflection are analogous, but reflective practice needs to be defined within the constraints of the subject matter. Reflective writing is a representation of reflection and not reflection itself. There are lots of ways to represent your reflections, but the representation is always a modified version and therefore more will be learnt. The more ways you represent it, the more you will learn:

> Learning is both a conscious and unconscious activity requiring the learner to process new information by drawing upon previous experience. This new information can only be applied to future situations if the learner is able to review and evaluate it, displaying an understanding and therefore gaining new knowledge. (McVittie, 2001)

Students began with journals that they designed and decorated. Boud et al. (1985) in Moon (2006) suggest that the journal is an extension of yourself and you must have ownership of it if it is to be a useful learning tool. Specific tasks were set in each session to develop reflection. These began with prompts that related directly to their experiences of the subject and were likely to start as descriptive:

- What is your personal experience of religion?
- Were you brought up within a faith? Was that a positive experience?
- What encounters have you had with other religions (travel, conversion, neighbours, friends, media)?
- How could your views of religion or of specific religions affect the way you teach RE?

Further into the module, the prompts focus on individual learning and analysis of experiences:

- Is this module or specialist theme what you expected? Why? Why not?
- Choose a session or activity you have particularly enjoyed. Write about it and explain why you enjoyed it.
- Choose a session or activity you found difficult or didn't enjoy. Write

about it and explain why you felt like this.
- How do you feel you are doing with the academic reading? Please read through the comments on your assignment and write down action points for improvements.

The journals were handed in at the end of each module and I acted as a critical friend. Extracts were also selected to share with peers. Initial recordings were very personal and inwardly focussed. The students appeared to be learning about themselves and how they viewed things in light of and sometimes in spite of events and experiences. It was evident from students' later entries that they were doing more than just describing an event, they were starting to analyse it and consider the reasons. There were also some changing perspectives and conclusions drawn following reflection on the reading tasks.

In addition to the prompts, students engaged in a number of creative tasks which were designed to allow creative responses. The introductory activities consisted of "a senses poem" and "a response to your world". Students were asked to go on a walk, run, train journey, anything where they could observe the environment. From these observations they had to produce a creative response. The following was a poem that was written on a train journey through differing landscapes:

It's Your World Too

Walking along the dirty street,
smiling softly at the people I meet,
funny looks and confused faces,
what an unhappy world this place is.

A good morning, a door held for you,
what must they want, what will they do?
Frightened people with suspicious minds,
thoughts racing through these troubled times.

Beautiful, flowing, clear rivers,
polluted by us like alcoholics' livers.
Innocent and pure, the minds of our children,
shattered and stolen by the world that we live in.

Where has my world gone? I feel like a fool,
destroyed by the humans for a measly stool.

Where have my family gone? Its such a shame,
hunted and killed, all part of a game.

This must stop.
It can't go on.
Before our beautiful world is finally gone.

(RE specialist 2006)

In a later session I used Philosophy for Children (P4C) to demonstrate how the activity and frame of reference can change your role in a group, encourage reflective and creative thinking.

I then asked the students to represent the P4C experience in their journals using pictures, symbols, writing, or a combination and to consider the following:

- the process
- being part of a group
- emotions
- having to speak in front of others

Students were constantly encouraged to work both within and outside their comfort zones in relation to preferred learning styles and reflective responses. Mind maps, flowcharts, and diagrams were used to promote alternative ways of expressing ideas. These session activities then supported the assessment which was in the form of a reflective portfolio and consisted of five individual pieces of creative reflection with a critical commentary relating to areas covered in the module and the learning objectives:

- Field trip response
- Digital story (responses from faith traditions to issues of global concern/beliefs in action)
- Awe and wonder and spirituality
- Personal and professional experiences of RE both in your own schooling and throughout this module

Figures 8-2 and 8-3 are examples of work included in the portfolio as a response to the awe and wonder and spirituality element. They are contrasting pieces with very different rationales. Student A wrote in the reflection:

Heaven is a vortex of wonder, no-one can be certain of what lies ahead after death. My poem represents what I believe Heaven is, Heaven is eternal happiness and if your place of happiness is a peaceful garden; a scenic coun-

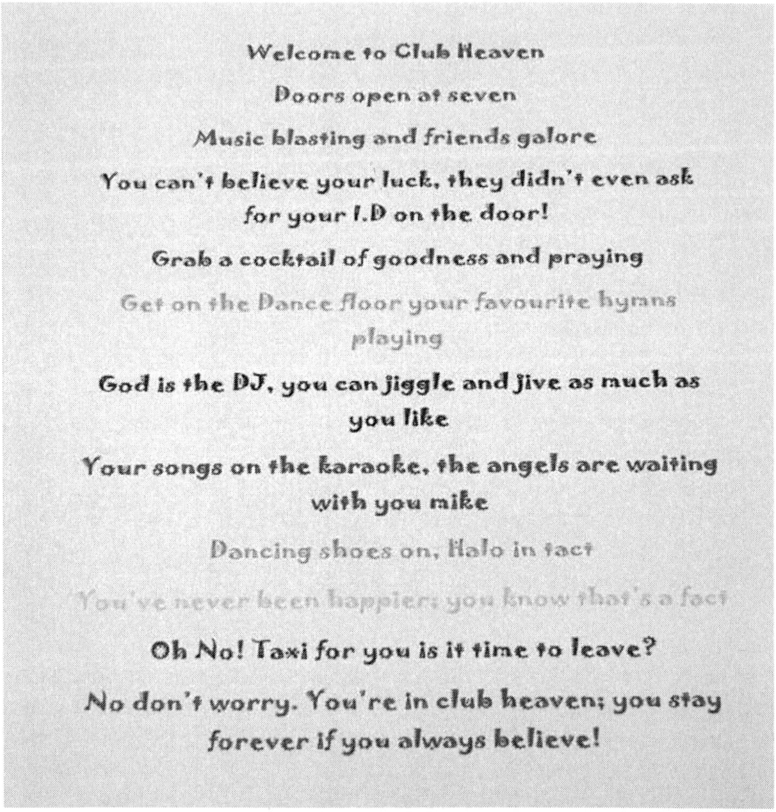

Fig. 8-2 (Student A)

> tryside setting or partying in an overcrowded club then your ideas will come true and be reflected in your Heaven.

The student was very clear in the rationale that she was in no way "mocking heaven or taking the concept and turning it into something that has comedy value". Student A was able to use this platform to express her thinking in a very emotive and open way which would not have been possible through a solely written response. Student B had a different approach:

> I never thought that a piece of children's work would spark that sense of wonder within me until I came across a poem written by an 8 year old boy. Through experience on my placement I have seen how wonder questions can have a positive impact upon the depth of thinking.

Fig. 8-3 (Student B)

Student B wanted to express thoughts about the wonder questions in her life but also to leave the piece open to interpretation and spark in the audience that sense of awe and wonder.

Figures 8-4 and 8-5 demonstrate responses to the personal and professional experiences element and both students have produced valid pieces. Student C's piece is very emotive:

> This bottle is my life. The stones represent all my experiences and encounters with RE and religion. The stones reach the age of 21, my age next month. I have put measuring lines on the bottle because I want to transmit that there is a lot of room left before the bottle is filled. I have had lots of experiences but I am going to have many more hopefully.

Student D, on the other hand, has approached the piece in a very logical manner as this was her strength according to the multiple intelligences section of the module:

> I see my learning as a flowing process as it seems to me that continuous

Fig. 8-4 (Student C)

> learning and experiences have flowed together and expanded my knowledge about different aspects of religious education. By including boxes such as a feeling box and a realisation box, it allowed me to express my emotions about certain aspects of experience and learning.

It was evident from the portfolios themselves and the student evaluations that this approach to RE made a difference to their thinking and allowed a variety of learning to take place which deepened through reflective practice.

> The focus on creativity has helped me to learn new things about myself that I didn't know I could do.

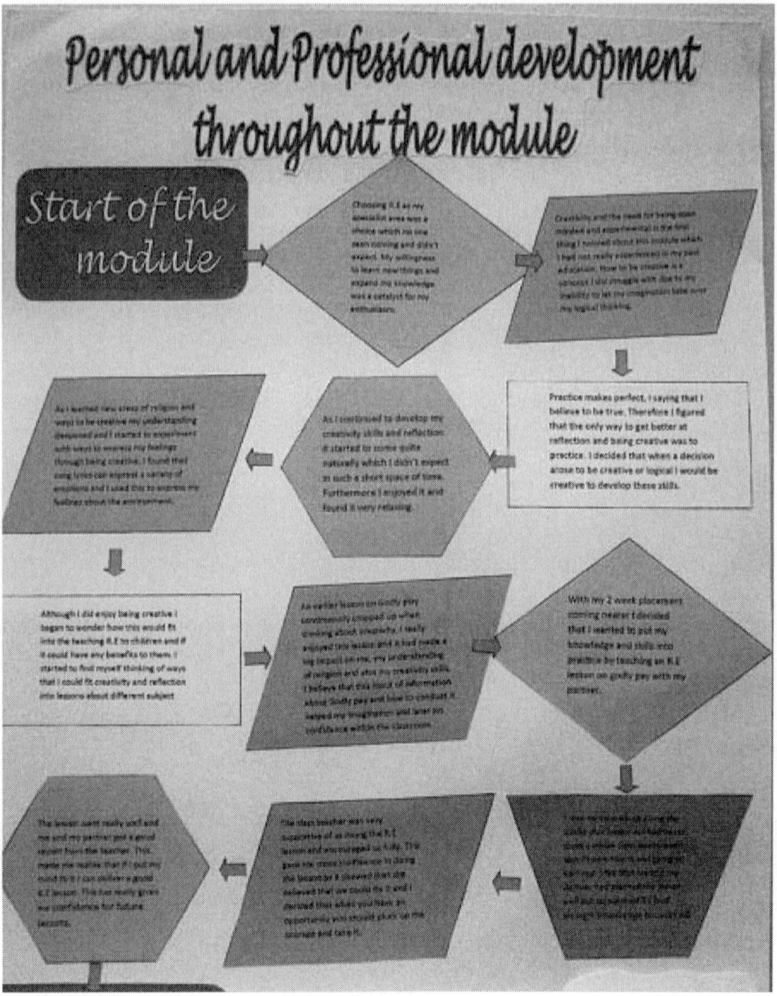

Fig. 8-5 (Student D)

The creative aspects in this module should be included more in the course for other students as it offers a variety of ways to display different thoughts and work.

Journals helped me understand more from the lesson and feel more confident about being reflective.

The Way Forward

Religious education is a complex subject and has faced many challenges on its journey and will undoubtedly face many more in the future. The rise in professionalism in RE in the 1930s brought with it concerns about the nature and teaching of religion in school on a local and world scale. These same issues are still being debated and discussed within the RE community. The context may have changed but the issues remain. Gates (2007) agrees that there has been under-provision in schools since at least 1944. According to Ofsted (2007) there is still a wide variation in provision and the subject generally depends upon the motivation and enthusiasm of the teacher. It is recognized that ITT provides limited training in many cases and this is not supplemented through continuing professional development once students qualify. Teacher educators involved in RE need to make the best use of their time with students and motivate them to want to learn more about this key subject. Engaging RE must consider the multifaceted nature of both the subject and the people who will ultimately teach it, one approach which may address this is through the use of creative teaching and learning in partnership with reflection. It allows students to be involved in the experience and therefore makes them better placed to take this forward in the classroom; and this, after all, is our goal.

References

Bakhtin, M. 1981. *The Dialogic Imagination.* Austin. University of Texas Press.

Boud, D., et al. 1985. *Reflection: Turning Experience into Learning.* London. Kogan Page.

DCSF. 2007. *Statutory Framework for the Early Years Foundation Stage.* London: Department for Children, Schools and Families.

Dewey, J. 1938. *Experience and Education.* New York. Simon and Schuster.

Ekebergh, M. 2007. 'Lifeworld-based Reflection and Learning: A Contribution to the Reflective Practice in Nursing and Nursing Education', *Reflective Practice*, 8(3): 331–43.

Erricker, C., and Costambeys, R. 2005. 'Bike Riding for Beginners: Living Difference and a Methodology for Teaching and Learning in RE', in *World Religions and Education.* London. Shap.

Gates, B. 2007. *Transforming Religious Education: Beliefs and Values under Scrutiny.* London. Continuum.

Hatton, N., and Smith, D. 1995. 'Reflection in Teacher Education: Towards Definition and Implementation', *Teaching and Teacher Education* 11(1): 33–49.

Howlett, D. 2009. 'Week 1: Creative and Effective Introduction', in *The Creative and Effective Curriculum.* Available at https://mylearning.cumbria.ac.uk. Accessed 10 November 2009.

McVittie, E. 2001. *Learning . . . as easy as 1, 2, 3?* Unpublished research. Edge Hill College.

Moon, J.A. 2004. *A Handbook of Reflective and Experiential Learning: Theory and Practice.* London. Routledge Falmer.

Moon, J.A. 2006. *Learning Journals: A Handbook of Reflective Practice and Professional Development.* 2nd ed. London. Routledge.

Ofsted. 2007. *Making Sense of Religion.* London. Ofsted.

Parahoo, K. 1997. *Nursing Research: Principles, Process and Issues.* Basingstoke. Macmillan.

QCA. 2004. *Religious Education: The Non-Statutory National Framework.* London. Qualifications and Curriculum Authority.

REC. 2007. *Commission Report: Religious Education Teaching and Training in England: Current Provision and Future Improvement.* London. Religious Education Council.

Rogers, C. 1969. *Freedom to Learn.* Columbus, OH. Charles E. Merrill.

Chapter Nine

Engaging with Christianity in Religious Education: Getting to the Heart of the Matter

Matthew Thompson

The worldwide revival of Islam has re-awoken consciousness of the vital power of religion in all aspects of life. Even in secular consciousness, religion has re-emerged as a key determinant in the pursuit of peace, justice, and harmony at all levels of community (local, regional, national, and international). This has been a rude awakening for those who slumbered for so long under the spell of secular world views that sought to confine the genius of religion into neat little spheres of individual and personal concern. A sound understanding of the nature of religions and the spiritual dimensions of life has never been so important for our collective welfare.

With its Christian heritage and identity, rooted in an established Church, the United Kingdom has long maintained religious education (RE) as a mandatory part of state education provision. In addition, in 1988 a government Act was passed which declared that every school must explicitly promote the spiritual development of its pupils. The transformation of the UK into a much more culturally and religiously diverse nation (and the challenges with respect to promoting a common foundation of values and purpose which can hold together that diversity as a true community) has afforded the opportunity for much debate over the resultant transformation of the aims, pedagogies, and outcomes of RE in our schools.

Nowhere is this more obvious than with respect to the teaching of Christianity and spiritual education. A recent report into the teaching of Christianity in secondary schools (Hayward, 2007) addresses the issue of pupil disengagement with this religion, relative to other (more recently and more exotically presented) religions taught in RE. The report recommends that RE should present Christianity as a living, "peopled", and global tradition. It offers a challenge to RE specialists to develop resources and pedagogies to promote a more engaging and realistic understanding of Christianity (Hayward, 2007: 90). An underlying issue here is a contempt bred by (a falsely assumed) over-familiarity with Christian tradition, which subsequently led to a tranquillization of Christian spirituality and its endless subjection to the brutal surgery of secular philosophical analysis. For decades now the Christian tradition has been wheeled out in UK schools by successive (increasingly secularized) RE syllabi, naked and anaesthetized before young, untrained RE students who are then handed the sharp instruments of secular philosophy to hack away in a vain search for an inner message whose very existence and veracity they are told they can thereby identify and judge.

Other religious traditions are usually presented in a more conscious form and their vital organs protected (for fear of offence) from the secular surgeon's knife (see Moran 2000). Nevertheless, the framework for that presentation is still a restricting, distorting, Western, secular, philosophical model. This will be illustrated with respect to the presentation of Christian tradition in and through "spiritual education".

In this paper, spirituality is defined as the fundamental force (expressed as wind or breath), orientation, and motivation that directs and drives the heart of a person, an organization, ideology or community.[1] This broad definition allows for the reality of evil and deceptive spirits as well as those which are good and true (and a great many between these two extremes). There is a broad consensus in Jewish, Christian, and Islamic tradition that the spirit (*ruach* or *ruh*) is associated with the very centre of a person, their heart. The soul (the operational centre of a person where the rational intellect is located) is in constant struggle to order the demands of our physical nature so that they can be of service to the driving spirit(s) within our heart. Whether implicit or explicit, conscious or unconscious, a driving spirit will always be present within any education institution and curriculum. As Wright concludes in his study of spirituality and education, "any viable critical education must be concerned with the search for ultimate spiritual truth" (Wright, 2000: 137).

This paper will examine the Western secular philosophical framework that has been driving the conception and presentation of the Christian faith and pupils' engagement with it in RE and spiritual education.

Testing the Spirit of Western Secular Spiritual Frameworks

Thatcher (1991) and Wright (1999) analysed the fundamental weakness of the philosophical "Western, liberal meta-narrative" that dominates contemporary educational philosophy and practice. That weakness is manifested in a vagueness and confusion that results from locating spiritual and religious truth in the subjective, inner experiences of the individual. For Wright, this is typified by what he calls the prevailing "experiential- expressive" model of religion, according to which all religions are presented as just culturally varying expressions of deep, inner spiritual experiences, anthropologically inherent within us all. Thatcher highlights the dangers of moral relativism that such a narrow, subjectivist philosophy breeds, reminding us how reducing the measure of truth to that which we make it opens the door to the justification of any kind of false and malicious standpoints (Thatcher, 1991: 25).[2]

Thatcher identifies the inadequacies of the narrow, distorting philosophical framework as lying in René Descartes' dualism, which distorts our idea of experience, reducing it to the inner feelings and mental states of an inner, private self. This has led Western philosophy (and education) down a long journey inwards into the self-obsessed liberal individualism and relativistic philosophies that govern contemporary educational (and much moral, political, and social) theory and practice. The subsequent neglect of communitarian elements is said to have been "fatally disabling" with respect to our understanding of religion and Christian spirituality. He contends that "The Biblical injunction to 'test the spirits to see whether they are of God' may well be applicable here"' (Thatcher, 1991: 23).

However, Thatcher ignores his own advice and instead takes (uncritical) recourse to the secular Western philosophical tradition of Wittgenstein with its critique of private language in order to refute this Western liberal metanarrative.[3]

Wright's analysis of the predominating philosophical framework is more extensive. Whilst he likewise identifies Cartesian dualism as a major cause of its inwardness, Wright also apportions blame to the Protestant theologian Friedrich Schleiermacher (1768–1834) and the Romantic Movement's assertion of the primacy of "inner spiritual experience" over outward, culturally determined "expressions" of religion. "Romanticism and the contemporary spiritual consensus . . . both advocate that we turn inwards and trust our own depths of spiritual experience, in order to encounter the heart of human existence" (Wright, 1999: 26).

Wright draws on the contemporary philosopher Gadamer's contention that

> the modern world as a whole is marked by an image of the individual turning inwards in order to discover truth: the scientific wing of modernity did this

> by relying on reason, the romantic wing of modernity by relying on feeling. Thus they represent two sides of the same coin. (1999: 26)

Wright points out that traditional Christian spirituality is grounded in the doctrine of original (or, it should be added, in Orthodox theology "ancestral") sin, with its insight that "the process of turning inwards and trusting inner feelings and experience leads not to God, *but to an encounter with the fallen nature of humanity. The trusting of inner feelings represents reliance not on divinity but on human corruption and sin*" (1999: 27, my emphasis).

Wright exposes the flaws of this inward-looking philosophical framework with respect to its inherent relativism, pointing out the danger that truth becomes regarded as unimportant, and as a result, "what really matters is the authenticity of our own inner experience. It is not what we believe that is the issue at stake, but the integrity and sensitivity of the ways we believe" (1999: 30).

However, at this most critical and insightful point of his analysis, Wright, like Thatcher, also withdraws from "testing the spirits" and has recourse to a secular philosophical framework (in his case, the obfuscating "critical realism" of R.A. Bhaskar with its "diverse approaches to truth" which incorporates the very secular, relativist and inward-looking approaches to truth whose flaws he had begun to expose. Ironically, Wright even expresses the foundation of his proposed alternative philosophical framework through a particularly Cartesian, inward-looking consideration that "our perceptions of the world are mistaken and . . . our lives are grounded in illusion" (1999: 34).

Like most RE specialists, Wright and Thatcher presume that presenting their subject matter through a secular philosophical framework (be it that of phenomenology, post-modernism, spiritual experientialism, critical realism, etc. – Grimmitt, 2000) facilitates both epistemological objectivity and moral, religious, and spiritual neutrality. This presumptuousness is characteristic of much secular Western educational philosophy and practice in general. It is symptomatic of the self-deception illustrated in the telling of the Indian story of the blind men and the elephant brought before the all-wise king. Each blind man grasps onto a different part of the elephant and falsely assumes he has understood the whole. The story is presented as a critique of any attempt on behalf of a faith or philosophy to lay claim to the Truth. But of course the deeper arrogance lies in those who identify with the all-seeing king who presumes to know, with imperial, absolute certainty, that what each man grasps is just a different part of the entire picture which only he, the mighty king, can see.

According to Christian tradition (and what later I will term its "sacred philosophy"[4]), secular Western philosophy cannot provide that all-seeing perspective because (as Wright hinted but then was unwilling to apply to himself) it is fundamentally rooted in the arrogant delusions of the fallen self. In this respect, Wittgensteinian language games and critical realism's "diverse approaches to truth" prove just as inward-looking and arbitrary. This means that they also are equally impotent in the face of moral, spiritual, and epistemological relativism which both dominates and undermines contemporary educational theory and practice. Therefore they are unable to form a framework fit to build an education system that can promote the insight and understanding into Christianity and spirituality which is so essential to the future development of our multicultural/faith communities. Secular philosophical frameworks do not provide epistemologically or morally neutral, "objective" foundations for religious and spiritual education. For example, in Wright's RE and spiritual education classrooms, holy and sacred spiritual traditions once again are to be wheeled in before students to be dissected by the blunt instruments drawn from his relativist toolbox of "diverse approaches to truth", which are thrust into the young school pupils' hands. According to Wright, those pupils thereby are allowed to "grapple for themselves with the conflicting and contrasting accounts of ultimate spiritual truth and value available in our pluralistic society" (1999: 39). The only prior training required is for pupils to "reflect upon" and "articulate" their own spirituality.

Wright claims that this pedagogical framework is a "hermeneutic of wisdom and suspicion" (1999: 39). However, from the perspective of Christian tradition, it constitutes another instance of elevating the subjective, individualized inner self to a position of supreme judge and arbiter of truth. In pedagogical terms it could be seen as equivalent in its naivety and potential for damage as thrusting untrained children into an operating theatre to perform major cardiac surgery.[5]

Christian tradition would be justified in asking Wright what had happened to that reverential holiness which earlier he had pointed out is so inseparable from the fundamental awareness of the fallen nature of the human self and which forms the fundamental beat at the heart of Christian spirituality.

Getting to the Heart of the Matter

I contend that the essential weakness of the secular philosophical framework is what might be called the Platonic/Cartesian doctrine of the "veil of appearance". This has been adopted, often unwittingly, by key players in the development of Western philosophical epistemology from Descartes, Locke, and Berkeley through to Hume, Kant, Ayer, and Wittgenstein (in both his so-called "early"' and his "later" philosophical stances). It is the assumption that all we ever directly perceive are our "ideas" (in the terminology of the philosophical Idealists) or "sense contents" (or similar such terms as favoured by Empiricists). Behind this epistemological and ontological veil of appearance, distinctions between appearance and reality, sensory experience and material object, subjective and objective experience, agency and necessity, morality and aesthetics (or psychology) all begin to break down. The individual subject, conceived either as the individual self (or else, as in Wittgenstein's language games, the linguistic community), is entombed within the solipsistic cave of his sensations or his linguistic community. Thus cut off from the consequently unknowable "outside" objective world, these "veiling" philosophies subsequently identify the boundaries of the objective world and objective truths with the boundaries of their solipsistic caves.

The consequence of being thus philosophically veiled can be seen in its corrosive effect upon the recognition of the reality of free-will, choice and agency. Common sense empiricist philosophers such as A.G.N. Flew (Flew and Vesey, 1987) have cogently demonstrated that acknowledgement of that reality logically assumes that we are placed very firmly in the world as active agents. Our ability to acquire, articulate, and question such terms and distinctions as, for example, "sensation" and "perception", "agency", "choice" and "necessity" is inseparable from their origin and affirmation in our everyday, shared experience as agents in a very real world. Those familiar with theodicy will be well aware that philosophers have long mistaken genuine choice or free-will to be synonymous with actions that are totally lacking in any kind of determination (Flew and Vesey, 1987; Thompson 1989). In effect, this mistake reduces the status of free-will and responsibility to mere unpredictable arbitrariness. The reality of genuine free-will resides in the fact the free agent is one who could have acted other than he in fact chose to act and this implies only the absence of physically necessitating causes and *not* the absence of causes in the sense of motivating reasons for the actual choice that was chosen. Flew's penetrating analysis of human rationality reveals that "The thesis of universal physical determinism could not even be understood by anyone who had not, in their experience of agency, had reason to know that it is false" (Flew and Thompson, 1987: 138).

The logic of rational and moral discourse also necessitates a fundamental assumption of our immersion in a shared (and unveiled) universal reality/experience.

Common sense empiricist philosophical tradition clearly identifies the distorted understandings of moral judgements that result from the elevation of the feelings, sentiments and accord of the individual subject to the status of logical as well as ontological ground of absolute value judgements. An essential component of the meaning of absolute moral value judgements is that they necessarily appeal beyond private sentiments and feelings peculiar to the individual making them and, in the words of Hume, that individual has to 'choose a point of view, common with him and others; he must move some universal principle of the human frame, and touch a string to which all mankind have an accord and symphony' (Hume, 1975: 272). Hume points out a consequence of attempting to ground absolute moral value judgement in the (more literally) self-centred and ultimately arbitrary desires, tastes, and sentiments of the individual self, namely, "the words, *honourable* and *shameful, lovely* and *odious, noble* and *despicable,* had never had place in any language; nor could the politicians, had they invented these terms, ever been able to render them intelligible, or make them convey any idea to the audience" (1975: 214, author's italics).

But neither can a solution be found through trying to ground those absolute value judgments in imaginary metaphysical realms of "synthetic a priori truths" (as with Kant and his categorical imperative; Kant, 1964) or Wittengenstein's mysterious "thatness" of the world (Wittgenstein, 1961 and 1965). These all prove to be equally insubstantial, arbitrary, and therefore ineffective foundations for absolute morality. They are manifestations of still being trapped (like Hume himself) behind, rather than remedies for, the veil of appearance. From behind this veil, it appears that all we ever directly perceive are our own subjective sensations, mere experiences (rather than actual perceptions) of a "reality", which is somehow always "out there" and, thereby, ultimately unknowable. Philosophy thus veiled moves inevitably from Truth to numerous "truths", from Good to myriad "goods", from the world to multiple "realities" (or Wright's "multiple world views"). Everything is reduced to a status, meaning, and value relative to the subject (conceived in multiple forms as either as individual person, age, gender, "race", "culture", language, etc.). The door is thus opened to all forms of divisive solipsistic discourses each of which blockades us within our own thoughts and ideas.

Even rationality inevitably is reduced to many different "concepts of rationality". However, as Flew points out,

> Certainly I can in thinking think only in terms of my own ideas. But this means no more than that in virtue of this my employment any idea which I employ becomes necessarily my idea. It does not mean that my concepts – whatever concepts, that is, I may happen to employ – cannot coincide with those of some other people. . . . Unless two cultures share at least some beliefs, and some ideas of truth and falsity and reality, then there can be no communication between them. (Flew, 1975: 95–96).

Flew illustrates this vital point as follows:

> Suppose we discover that the Kachin word previously rendered "rationality" in fact refers to a wholly different concept, then this merely shows that we have been mistranslating. Suppose that the two terms are perfectly equivalent, then we have no alternatives to choose between. It is only if, though they are not perfectly equivalent, that they do have a great deal in common that we are warranted to speak of two concepts of rationality. But to object now to the insistence that what they have in common – what makes them both concepts of rationality – *is* rationality is to align yourself with old Marshall Saxe. It was he who, according to legend, wanted reassurance that the planet which we call Uranus really *is* Uranus. (1975: 97, author's emphasis)

We can conclude therefore that behind the veil of appearance, disputes about truth and attempts to resolve them are ultimately rendered insoluble, being reduced to initiations into different "ways of seeing the world". Contradictions and disputes between such diverse ways of seeing and their competing truth claims are rendered immune to rational argument, allowing relativism to reign supreme, thereby opening the door to its inevitable reduction of right to might. The truth of knowledge and belief claims is reduced to the subjective states in which they are held (Thompson, 1989: chapters 3 and 4).

Christian Sacred Philosophy

Christian tradition offers a deeper diagnosis of (and remedy for) the flawed inward-looking, relativistic secular philosophy that so dominates contemporary educational theory and practice. The primary sources for this Christian tradition are its sacred scripture and sacred Church tradition. The following analysis draws primarily on the foundation text of all sacred Scripture, the book of Genesis, but also the metaphorical imagery of the "garden of the heart" derived from that primary source and developed in medieval Catholic tradition in, for example, the thirteenth- or twelfth-century *Book of Virtues and Vices/Somme le Roi* (Thompson, 1997). The philosophy that lies at the heart of Christian tradition will henceforth be referred as "sacred philosophy".[6]

This sacred philosophy traces the origins of the flawed philosophical framework back to the very beginning of humanity's struggle with truth and reality, as revealed in the book of beginnings, Genesis. Chapter 3 of Genesis recounts Adam's Satanically induced rejection of the ultimate source of all truth, namely, the revelation of the Divine Word. This leads Adam into the erroneous deception that individual human reason (conceived in the restricted form of the subjectivized human word) is the sufficient and supreme source of truth. It is this subjectivized, naturalistic/humanistic understanding of our experience that then seeks to squeeze God (and reality) into a veiled, inward, private realm. Sacred philosophy reveals that in the very beginning and also at the very end of any agonizing, authentic debate about truth, each one of us stands in the midst of the garden of our heart facing an ultimate choice: do we hearken to the voice (Word) of divine revelation (that blessed Hebrew command "Hear"/"shema" – Deuteronomy 6.4), or do we make our self (our own, "naturalized" human word) supreme?

It is in what we might term this "garden of the heart" that two opposing views of knowledge, truth and philosophy take root, the one claiming "Man is the measure", the other declaring that "the fear of the Lord is the beginning of wisdom". Sacred philosophy contends that the former dooms the subject to operate forever as a spectator hidden behind a veil of appearance, the supreme god of his own ultimately lonely, isolated universe which he then has to imbue with (ultimately subjective, contingent, and arbitrary) meaning, value, and purpose. The latter promises to liberate the individual to be a co-agent, operating firmly within and upon divine creation.

If the latter choice is taken, then the prime and most authoritative philosophical text is the divine Word/Logos revealed in both its written and living forms. For those choosing the primordial Protagorean route, recourse to such authority may appear, at first sight, foolishness and/or a stumbling block (1 Corinthians 1–2).

According to sacred philosophy, the heart is the very centre of the person, the locus of our identity, our deepest desires, values, sense of purpose, our direction, dignity, choice, responsibility and hence the dwelling place of the spirit that drives it. Sacred philosophy asserts, "For as he thinketh in his heart, so is he" (Proverbs 23.7). The heart is the location for what emerges as the greatest, most vital battle to be fought in the entire history of the human race, the spiritual battle for the soul. This is the battle for the most vital decisions, orientation, purpose, value, and direction in our life and hence the key determinant of our understanding of development and education.

In the beginning of beginnings (Genesis 1–2), Wisdom is presented as the divine creative Intellect, synonymous with the divine Word (Proverbs 8.23–31) and is manifest in the very heart of creation (conceived as the Garden of Eden) in the Tree of Life planted there. Humanity (Adam) is also presented there as a living being, very much in and of the earth (Hebrew *adama* meaning "earth" as well as "mankind"), and as an active agent with a divinely bestowed dignity and appointed role as active lord with responsibility to "dress" and "keep" the garden (Genesis 2.15). There is no veiling of a so-called "external" reality behind any Platonic/Cartesian type of subjective appearances. Human purpose and fulfilment (the key drivers of any education system) were not to be found merely in the detached intellectual philosophical musings of a spectator, but rather through creative agency within and upon that reality and so help to bring forth its fruits. This garden of the heart of creation in which man is placed is mirrored in the creative heart that lies within each and every individual human, in which also there is planted the living seed of divine wisdom and a divinely appointed duty to dress and keep (protect) it. Therefore, sacred philosophy is inherently practical (virtue-based) in its conception and application and hence eminently suitable to provide the framework for developing educational theory and practice.

The substantial reality of the divinely bestowed responsibility, dignity, purpose, value, and direction that lies within this heart is contingent upon the substantial reality of mankind's autonomy, free-will, or choice. In sacred philosophy, this substantial reality is represented (or directly *presented*) by the second tree planted in the centre of the heart, the Tree of Knowledge of Good and Evil (Genesis 2.9).

The locus of this free-will/choice is the heart of the person, not the intellect. The intellect provides the tools for weighing up means to ends (and thus consequences), but the initial choice of (and responsibility for) direction is firmly grounded in the heart alone. Hence the presence of the two trees in the centre of the garden of the heart. The consequences of each of the alternative choices are clearly presented by the Divine Word as being utterly ultimate in nature (life or death), further adding gravitas to the reality and responsibility of that choice (and free-will). However, the fact that this primordial (yet equally ultimate) choice cannot be made by the intellect does not reduce that choice to mere arbitrariness. It is a choice governed (but not physically necessitated) by the degree to which the subject makes his/her heart receptive, open and obedient to the divine Word.

It is important to reiterate that this does not imply that the choice is somehow irrational. Appeal to rationality is made on behalf of both of the alternatives. It is an easy mistake to infer from the presence of the two trees in the garden that man (Adam) in his pre-fallen, innocent state was pre-rational, semi- or sub-conscious, and that avoiding eating the only tree forbidden to him would maintain him in a state of blissful ignorance. The error of this inference is made clear by the assertion that Adam was already imbued with ample awareness and knowledge to name (to be fully conscious of, understand, classify, and have dominion over) the other living creatures (Genesis 2.19–20). So the ultimate and primordial choice is not that between either rationality/full-consciousness or semi-conscious, naive animal-like *a*rationality. Rather it is between on the one hand reason/rationality directed solely Godward and on the other, reason/rationality directed to the individual self.

Part of secular, agnostic philosophical tradition also has recognized that in making our most ultimate, absolute value judgements, "Reason is and ought only to be the slave of the passions" (Hume, 1911: 2.127), that "something must be desirable on its own account, and because of its immediate accord or agreement with human nature or sentiment" (Hume 1975: 293) and that "morality . . . is more properly felt than judged of" (Hume, 1911: 2.178). This talk of deep accord, feeling and sentiment represents a secular philosophical insight into the central role of the human heart as revealed in the sacred philosophy. Hume also discerned that absolute value judgements cannot logically be derived from propositions expressing matters of fact and real existence (the logical impossibility of deriving an "ought" from an "is" statement).

According to sacred philosophy, without the divine Word, that "accord, feeling and sentiment" amounts to no more than contingent (and ultimately arbitrary) fact about the individual subject. This gives rise to the Satanic, self-deifying delusion of philosophical relativism and subjectivism, namely, that, ultimately, it is the individual subject/self that is the very ground, foundation and magisterial imbuer of all value and truth in the world.

Conclusion: Consequences for Religious Education

The pedagogical consequences of all this for RE obviously are important. The ultimate claims and demands of Christian religion and spirituality cannot effectively be encountered, understood, or taught through any secular Western philosophical framework that has usurped the authority of God with that of the fallen self. Religions and their spiritualities can only be truly understood when presented in their living and lived out fullness. In practice this means encountering those awesomely powerful genii of the faiths. Expecting students to engage in authentic philosophical analysis of the nature and veracity of these genii is like throwing them into a lion's den or a wrestling ring with Goliath. Religions bite! They make the most ultimate claims and demands possible. By definition, religions bind us together, yet they can also rip us apart. If RE demands serious encounter with living faith rather than anaesthetized surgical cases wheeled in by secular philosophy, then serious thought needs to be given to developing appropriate pedagogies, including some substantial protective headgear (to avoid damage from the bigotry and fanaticism that inevitably will be encountered).

This returns us to Hayward's call for more engaging teaching of Christianity through presenting it as a living, "peopled", and global tradition and her challenge to RE specialists to develop "resources and pedagogies to promote a more engaging and realistic understanding of Christianity" (Hayward, 2007: 90). An authentic engagement with Christian belief (and an understanding of what it means to the believer) necessarily demands some form of exploration and understanding of the fundamental, primordial challenge it presents to the human heart (the same could be said with respect to authentic encounter and engagement with all the living religious traditions studied in RE). This in turn necessitates breaking out of the restricting and distorting secular philosophical framework that dominates and controls our educational establishments. The first stage in this task is to increase awareness of the (all-pervasive and controlling) existence and nature of this secular framework, revealing it to be incapable of providing the epistemological, moral, or spiritual objectivity and neutrality which its adherents have falsely assumed. Once this awareness has been achieved, it is then possible to facilitate an authentic encounter with the heart (and hence the real ground of human spirituality), but no longer (as with the secular philosophical framework) from the perspective of an isolated "self" veiled from myriad "realities" and "truth". This secular philosophical framework condemns our learners to be "ever learning and never able to come to knowledge of the truth"'(2 Tim. 3.7). Understanding sacred philosophy has the potential to liberate learners and enable them to encounter the heart of our humanity as a person rooted in a common reality and genuine community.

Appendix

Over recent years Liverpool Community Spirit (LCS) has been developing and applying pedagogical techniques and educational resources for the classroom (including adult learners) to promote awareness of and engagement with some of the key principles of this sacred philosophy and, thereby, some of the realities and challenges of the Christian faith. For example, a short DVD retelling Genesis 3, the Fall of Adam and Eve (but including Satan's earlier "fall") set in a contemporary Liverpool context was written, produced, and directed with the help of LCS Youth Council members and volunteers from diverse communities in Toxteth, Liverpool. Teacher resources and activities engaging learners in exploring key concepts such as choice, responsibility, good, evil, and sin (as well as God, creation, and Satan) have been trailed in local prisons (as part of LCS' Faith Diversity Training courses) and also (through partnership with Liverpool Hope University's RE PGCE Department) KS 4 and 5 students in Liverpool schools. These materials make both implicit and explicit links between the fundamental challenges presented by Christian sacred philosophy within the universal context of the Garden of Eden and the personal, individual context of the "garden" of our own human heart. They have proven to be a particularly useful means of providing a fresh and stimulating encounter with the realities of the Christian faith, through pedagogical techniques focussing upon learners' faculties of personal reflection, analysis and interpretation, whilst at the same time providing a neutral, "safe and secure" investigative context that avoids any potential compromise of the educational integrity of RE.

The DVD (which also explores the challenges of the seven deadly sins in contemporary settings) is available from Liverpool Community Spirit (www.community-spirit.org.uk). Some of the accompanying teacher resource materials were demonstrated through an interactive workshop at the Hope University colloquium on Engaging RE and also will be available from LCS late in the year.

Notes

1 An earlier exploration and elaboration of this definition of spiritual education can be found in Thompson, 1997.

2 Copley (2000) rightly attributes this domination to the post-1945 growth in multiculturalism and the abandonment of the Christian confessional framework of RE in favour of a multifaith format. But he appears to welcome the resultant confusion as an opportunity "to take seriously" the second of the two attainment targets that still control the assessment and subsequent presentation of RE in UK schools, namely, learning about religion and learning from religion.

3 Thatcher takes (uncritical and apparently secondhand) recourse to merely asserting (rather than arguing) the validity of the secular Western philosophical tradition of Wittgenstein and his critique of private language and subjectivity (Thatcher, 1991: 23 and his footnote reference to A. Kenny, 1984).

4 Assuming a broad definition of philosophy as the struggle (intellectual and practical) to articulate the key categories of our human framework of understanding (and therefore as inseparable from spirituality as defined above), the term "sacred philosophy" is used here to refer exclusively to the Christian framework for understanding as contained in sacred scripture and apostolic tradition).

5 The philosophical contradictions inherent within Wright's pedagogical framework and the consequent dangers of throwing untrained pupils into the theatre of major philosophical surgery, are manifest in the attempt by Susanna Hookway to apply Wright's pedagogical framework, with its "critical realist" approach to truth, to the classroom (Hookway, 2004). Teachers are given a very confusing (yet thereby, for our context, revealing) description of a "theistic approach to truth" that, according to Hookway, "maintains that there is a divine reality, truth 'out there'" (2004: 4) the inverted commas are, revealingly, Hookway's). Her inclusion of the term "truth" in this statement lends an ambiguity to her subsequent assertion that to "maintain that the truth in which they believe is unequivocally correct" is "a fundamentalist stance" (2004: 4). Hooker, following Wright, wants to have her cake and eat it: on the one hand, to claim that their epistemology (and pedagogy) is "realistic" in that they acknowledge the existence of an objective reality (moral and ontological) about which religions make (competing and often incompatible) truth claims. On the other hand, they also wish to resort to talk of different "truths" as different ways of seeing the world/truth, between which there can be no room for rational discourse, but, ultimately, only subjective choice. Hookway naively expects pupils to decipher which of a list of statements which she describes as different "truths" (inverted commas, again revealingly, are Hookway's) can be demonstrated as true by using scientific reason (2004: 8, 13). The only tools they (and their teacher) are given to do this task are Hookway's three short (simplistic and misleading) paragraph summaries of three so-called "approaches to truth", together with an equally simplistic and misleading one-line definition of "absolute", "relative" and "verifiable" truth. Surely it should be pointed out that if this analysis is to be meaningful and authentic, it requires proper tools and training, including understanding the nature and difference between key categories such as statements of fact and statements of value; analytical and synthetic truths, a priori and a posteriori truths, different types of cause, etc. More disturbing is Hookway's presentation of the

"truths" (inverted commas mine) about the conflict in Jerusalem and, by extension, Israel. This is an explosive and sensitive topic the clear understanding and presentation of which lies at the very heart of present concerns over religious violence and community cohesion both nationally and internationally. RE is sometimes given the awesome responsibility to help pupils address this issue through sensitive and informed understanding. However, Hookway's materials, whilst claiming to present an "objective" presentation of two sides of a debate, actually display a clear disparity in the presentation of the claims to land of two opposing sides (Muslim/Arab and Jewish/Israeli), which includes only one personal (Arab) story which describes Jews in inflammatory terms (presented by Hookway as innocent "facts") as "Zionist forces, who wanted to purify the land of Palestinian people" (2004: 40).

6 The term "sacred philosophy" as employed in this paper has no connotations of, nor should be seen as in any way synonymous with nor related to, any kind of Gnostic, Perennial, Universal, Transcendent sacred philosophy as conceived in any non-exclusively Christian context.

References

Bhaskar, R. A. 2008. *A Realist Theory of Science*. 2nd ed. London. Verso.

Copley, T. 2000. *Spiritual Development in the State School: A Perspective on Worship and Spirituality in the Education System of England and Wales*. Exeter. University of Exeter Press.

Flew, A.G.N. 1975. 'Anthropology and Rationality', *Question*, 5.

Flew, A.G.N. 1978. *A Rational Animal*. Oxford. Clarendon Press.

Flew, A.G.N., and Vesey, G. (eds). 1987. *Agency and Necessity*. Oxford. Basil Blackwell.

Grimmitt, M. (ed.). 2000. *Pedagogies of Religious Education*. Great Wakering. McCrimmons.

Hayward, M. 2007. *Christianity in Religious Education at Key Stage 3*. Warwick Religions and Education Research Unit Occasional Paper IV. Warwick. University of Warwick.

Hookway, S. 2004. *Questions of Truth: Developing Critical Thinking Skills in Secondary Religious Education*. Norwich. Religious and Moral Education Press.

Hume, D. 1911. *A Treatise of Human Nature*. 2 vols. London. Dent. (Originally published 1740.)

Hume, D. 1975. *Inquiries Concerning Human Understanding and Concerning the Principles of Morals*. Reprinted from the 1777 edition with introduction and analytical index by L.A. Selby-Bigge. 3rd ed. Oxford. Clarendon Press.

Kant, I. 1964. *Groundwork of the Metaphysics of Morals*. Translated and analysed by H.J. Paton. New York. Harper and Row. (Originally published 1785.)

Kenny, A. 1975. *Wittgenstein*. Harmondsworth. Penguin Books.

Moran, P. 2000. *Let Me Teach RE, Not Someone's Ideology! Reflections on How Multicultural Concerns have been Shaping Religious Education*. www.islamatschool.org.uk/GC/GCSETopicsPages/Articles.htm. Accessed 6

March 2008.
Thatcher, A. 1991. 'A Critique of Inwardness in Religious Education', *British Journal of Religious Education,* 14(1): 22–27.
Thatcher, A. (ed.). 1999. *Spirituality and the Curriculum*. London. Cassell.
Thompson, M.G. 1989. *The Problem of Good in the Problem of Evil: A Thesis Concerning Supernatural Religion*. Unpublished PhD thesis, Dept. Of Theology, University of Birmingham, England.
Thompson, M.G. 1997. *Spiritual Education: The Seed of English Renaissance*. Llantwit Major. United World College of the Atlantic.
Wittgenstein, L. 1961. *Tractatus Logico-Philosophicus*. London. Routledge and Kegan Paul.
Wittgenstein, L. 1965. 'Wittgenstein's Lecture on Ethics', *The Philosophical Review LXXIV*.
Wittgenstein, L. 1966. *Lectures and Conversations on Aesthetics, Psychology and Religious Belief*. Edited by C. Barrett. Oxford. Basil Blackwell.
Wright, A. 1993. *Religious Education in the Secondary School: Prospects for Religious Literacy*. London. David Fulton.
Wright, A. 1999. *Discerning the Spirit: Teaching Spirituality in the Religious Education Classroom*. Abingdon. Culham College Institute.
Wright, A. 2000. *Spirituality and Education*. London. Routledge Falmer.

Chapter Ten

Notes on a Catholic Spirituality of Christian Education

Daniel O'Leary

This paper attempts to recover a Catholic vision of Christian education. It is an effort to restore a spiritual heart to schools where the pursuit of academic success is becoming the main agenda. It then attempts to apply the implications of this vision to that point in Christian education where the work of teaching and of catechizing overlap. I begin with the suggestion that all teaching and catechizing is based on a theology. And it is important that we should be able to articulate that theology. Otherwise we do not have a ground to stand or build on. The theology of Vatican Council II is both imaginative and sacramental. It offers a vision of creation and incarnation that brings a new dynamism to our ministry in the classroom and the parish room.

The Catholic tradition explored in this paper is based on an orthodox theology of nature and grace. It provides a much-needed balance to a largely misunderstood theology of sin and redemption which has encouraged Catholics, for centuries, to fall into a deadly pattern of dualism. Dualism is a kind of heresy which separates the sacred from the secular, the holy from the profane. It arises from a deeply flawed grasp of the doctrine of original sin, with devastating consequences for Christian education. A theology of nature and grace, on the other hand, being radically incarnational, sees God's presence in all humanity and in all creation. This sacramental vision, this Catholic imagination, profoundly reshapes the content and the aims of our religious education and catechetical endeavours.[1]

This chapter touches on some of these issues, providing some notes and pointers towards the nature and implications of this interpretation of revelation. This rediscovered approach has always been an essential, but too often neglected, dimension of the Catholic tradition. It brings a richness and a resonance that gives new life to our efforts to truly educate young people in the Christian faith. Throughout the reflections that follow, suggestions are made for linking this sacramental imagination, this theological vision with an experience-based, life-centred educational theory in a results-dominated age.

Much creative work needs to be entered into before we can restore to the young and old of our schools and parishes this central spiritual vision and imagination. Many questions arise. How can hearts be touched? How can faith be "caught"? How do we protect and liberate that innate creativity already inside our students, waiting to be drawn out? How do we make both relevance to life and abundance of humanity the aim of all our teaching and catechizing?

One way is by paying more attention to the hearts and minds of those who work so generously and faithfully in our schools and parishes. Too often the prescribed books and programmes do not touch the source of all transformation – the spirit, enthusiasm, and motivation of the educator. The heart of catechesis is the heart of the catechist. The teacher's spirit must be transformed before the students' will be. "Unless the faith means something to the teacher," Cardinal Hume used to say, "it will not mean much to the student."

It is time to restore to people once again what belongs to them, by virtue of their birth and baptism – that is, their idealistic fire, their divine light and unique loveliness. Maybe we need to re-romanticize faith and religious education, to give our students something beautiful to fall in love with.

One thing must be noted. Given the continually changing nature of the world we live in, a mere adaptation of what worked in the past may not be enough. Maybe another renaissance is needed – a renaissance of the sacramental imagination. The use of those words should not put us off. Imagination, sacramentality, and faith have always been sisters. Imagination is the divine creativity within us. The way we faithfully co-create our lives and the world with God depends on the vitality of our imagination, in the Catholic vision. Such imaginative vision needs to be nourished through exposure to the arts, to the great stories of the world, to intimate conversations with ourselves and with others, to play and to children, to poetry and to music, and to everything that nurtures our intuition and our sensitivity to God's presence all around us. Without catching the vision, the heart does not know where to go; but without the fire of imagination it doesn't want to go anywhere, least of all to church!

More than a Duty

The General Directory for Catechesis integrates theology, spirituality, and catechesis. It hopes for a profound transformation of mind and heart, by nourishing the depths of the human person in everything that he or she is

(Catholic Church. Congregation for the Clergy, 1998: 55, 57). We hope that our teaching and catechizing will carry a spiritual energy, a life-force, to deepen our hearers' grasp of the world, and of their own lives, and of all that is happening in them.

In our schools and parishes we wonder if it is a reasonable and legitimate goal to aim for, that students of all ages, and from all cultures and backgrounds, will become wise enough to make more sense of the darkness and light within them, to live more abundantly, and to fall in love more deeply with the God of their lives and of their world. Do we really believe that our work with others is primarily to engender in them a passion for the possible, a devotion to liberating all who are unjustly oppressed, to serve the needy, to be transformed radically into courageous prophets and risk-takers?

Given the legitimacy of these aims and hopes, is there a skilled methodology to facilitate this transformation? In the marvellous light of a powerful and positive theology, how do we restructure and re-vision our approaches to the process of evangelizing and catechizing? Or do we first need to learn how to set the hearts of our teachers on fire with the vision? Michael Himes quotes St Augustine's desire for enthusiasm and enjoyment on the part of the teacher and catechist. They need these graces so as to "not only teach others – in order to instruct them; not only to delight them – in order to hold them; but also to sway them – in order to conquer and win them." (Himes, 2006: 114) Teaching is also about delighting and persuading. In recent years, when talking to pastoral ministers of the gospel, Cardinal Murphy O'Connor (Westminster) and Archbishops Martin (Dublin) and Williams (Canterbury) have used phrases like "being on fire", "being passionate", "being totally committed to", and "being broken and remade by the vision" so as always to be witnesses to God's free love and self-giving.

Content in Catechesis

There are many questions and issues around this whole topic – too many for consideration here. Volumes have been written about the place of "knowledge" and "experience" in educational content.

The story of RE and catechetics in England and Wales often revolves around this issue of "content in the curriculum". How can "human experience" be regarded as "content"? If the very essence of students' lives is regarded, by an incarnational theology, as the subject-matter of revelation, how can Christian educational guidelines focus on, explore, and sustain that very essence and those experiences, in such a way as to reveal to the students the sacredness of their lives? The Catholic hierarchy is always keen that objective knowledge should be passed on. Can this understandable objective go hand in hand with a more creative, poetic and experiential understanding of the faith – one that provides for the "catching" of the imaginative vision of creation and humanity, "the mind of Christ"?

There is one non-negotiable insight to hold on to in all our reflecting and debating. That is, the grace of God has always been there, ahead of our preaching and teaching. These activities are not some kind of indoctrination with something from outside but the awakening of something within, as yet not understood but nevertheless really present. We are born into the world in the warmth of God's love which never leaves us. A theology which perceives an integral relation between revelation and life-experience will view the educational procedure largely in terms of process and development where the student is seen as unique in her personal growth and becoming.

It is precisely around the "skill" of entering confidently into this vision and process that much of the anxiety and uncertainty among our teachers and catechists is found today. A renewed spiritual perception is now increasingly essential for bringing about a deepening understanding of the aims and work of Catholic education.

First there is the provision of occasions for students to reflect on what they have seen, done, learnt, suffered, and enjoyed. There is the drawing out from them how they reacted to those experiences, the meaning they gave to them, the emotions they felt. Then there is the reviewing and consideration of this exercise in the light of Christian revelation about the deeper personal and universal significance of all life's experiences. Some obvious questions arise here. What part of this special work can be achieved in the more formal setting of structured sessions? How can people, in any setting, be brought to the limits of their own creativity and imagination, to the "moment of disclosure"? How can they, in the light of incarnation, be enabled to decode, to interpret their own mystery?

If the loving relationship between God and humanity is seen as something that goes beyond a body of truths into the deeper realms of the interpersonal, the experiential and the historical, then the concern of Christian education will be to express that relationship in a language, and through a catechetical method, that is in touch with people's present, personal experience of the love and meaning in the essence of their lives.

Head and Heart Together

A central concern is to ensure that none of the traditional contents of the Catholic faith is overlooked in our presentation of a renewed Christian vision. It is important to clarify that in the overall "content" of our "handing on" of the faith, there is no necessary conflict between the place of human experience and the place of the doctrines of our tradition. The "content" of our lived experiences on the one hand, and that of the knowledge of Scripture and Tradition on the other, can never be over against each other, as though they were in competition for pride of place. Like nature and grace, they go, and grow, together. Revealed truth cannot work against itself.

The accurate and balanced grasp of the meaning of revelation, of the sacramental vision at the heart of incarnation, provides the context and contours of our approaches to any kind of faith mission. How we perceive the tangible nature of incarnation and redemption, and how we are personally transformed by it, will radically colour our motives and methods in sharing the Good News with our students. Getting the vision clear, and then the tactics for realizing it, is a crucial challenge for those responsible for the faith development of young and old today. The Christian teacher works towards the faith-horizon that sees the mystery of the incarnation as revealing the hand and heart of God already and always at work in the daily life of each person, and of the universe itself.

Michael Himes refers to Cardinal Newman's *An Essay in Aid of a Grammar of Assent* where he distinguishes between "notional assent" (the acceptance of the truth of an inference) and "real assent" (the acceptance of an experience). Himes writes:

> Communicating faith is not primarily a matter of supplying propositions and information (although that is part of faith) but rather evoking and naming experiences. The teacher of faith should help his hearers examine their experience and offer categories to them for understanding that experience. Teaching faith is, in a sense, offering people a hermeneutic for interpreting what they experience within and around themselves so that disparate parts of their experience begin to connect and emerge as a meaningful whole. (Himes, 2006: 122)

Information and Transformation

There are many challenges facing the teacher and catechist as they present and balance their material for the students. On the one hand there are the more formal marks of the faith-life such as a knowledge of Church doctrines and of Scripture, sacramental and devotional practice, and, on the other, the actual experience of that salvation, that union with God in Christ, in the here and now. Clarity in this matter will have much impact on the vision and tactics deployed in the educational work of faith schools and in the way it is received by the students.

Because we are dealing with divine/human mystery here, there will never be one perfect approach. Maybe the whole enterprise of a liberating transmission of a vibrant sacramental vision is a mixture of many "contents", "presences" and processes –

- the appropriate subject-matter or formal knowledge;
- the central place of the "raw material" of actual experience to be interpreted;
- the hope of preparing a readiness for a deeper, transforming understanding of life in the future;
- the thorough, personal conviction of the teacher about the wonder and beauty of insights they endeavour to instil; and
- the powerful influence of the wider Christian community – e.g. family and parish – in the formation of the young soul.

The real content of our endeavours is not only the knowledge, facts, information about the faith – in themselves; it is about how they reveal God's secret about life itself. And not life in an abstract, philosophical sense, but life as it is lived and experienced by child and adult alike, seeking and discovering, right here and right now, an abundance and a transformation in their deepest humanity, through an intimacy with the Son of God, the Human One.

In broad outline there is a teaching strategy that seems to fit the vision of a theology of nature and grace. Arising from the basic "nature/grace" movement within such a theology, it seems appropriate to have three fundamental phases in an appropriate educational pattern. The first phase looks at aspects of personal experience, creation, and the human condition (nature). After the creative exploring by the students of these aspects and experiences, the second phases is the transforming light shed on them by the birth and Passover of Jesus Christ (grace) is then revealed. This is the good news, the spiritual awakening, that changes everything. The third phase is where the new awareness of this deeper love and meaning at the heart of students' lives and loves (the "new creation") is constantly purified, persevered in, delighted in, and celebrated in all kinds of ways. This is the awareness that motivates and empowers the students with a sense of mission and service to the world.

Intrinsic Model

The structure of most of our current syllabuses is prone to a persistent flaw which betrays a misunderstanding of the real meaning of incarnation. This flaw usually shows itself in one of two ways. The use of human experience in a renewed design (often referred to as a "life-theme") is not meant to be a way of capturing the students' interest before bringing in the explicitly "religious knowledge" dimension at the end, nor is the human experience content meant to be the self-contained locus of "implicitly" religious values, carrying *within itself alone* the revelation of its own meaning. Rather an *intrinsic* model seeks to maintain, within the life-theme design, the integrity of both the "sacred" and the "secular" elements of experience. This has to be so because the experience explored in the life-theme constitutes that basic condition for Christian revelation which can be mediated *only in terms* of that human experience.

That is why, in this renewed life-centred design, the initial exploration into human experience as we generally have it today in schools across the country is not to be regarded as a kind of preamble to some central religious input, but is, *in itself* (and only in itself, in *this* time, place and person) the necessary locus that is refined and purified, enlightened, and humanized, saved, and perfected, by the new design of love as revealed in Christ. This visionary approach will view the educational procedure more in terms of process and development in a dialectical curriculum model. The student is seen as unique in her personal growth and becoming, and all the factors involved in this process are recognized and acknowledged as intrinsic to her understanding, acceptance and experience of a personal, dynamic and divine revelation.

Integrating Sacred and Secular

"Experience", then, should not be considered as an additional, preliminary "content-area" for catechesis or religious education. Rather it constitutes the existential condition for God's saving action to be revealed in every detail of our lives. The task and privilege of the teacher and catechist is to bring the image of God, already incontrovertibly secure at the core of each human's life and of the life of the world, to the edge of their experience – ever closer, as St Paul reminds us, to the shining likeness of God, through the medium of knowledge and formation in the graced beliefs, rituals, and daily lives of the Christian community. This is where we find the Catholic imagination, the sacramental vision, at its best.

The Sacred and the Secular

> The first and most obvious problem is how to construct curricula that can be taught by ordinary teachers to ordinary pupils and that at the same time reflect clearly the basic underlying principles of various fields of inquiry. (Bruner, 1960: 98)

In addressing similar issues within the world of Christian education, there are certain theological underpinnings that the catechist or teacher needs to keep always in mind. The new consciousness that has transformed the meaning of being human springs from the truth that God has created, and then assumed (in Christ), the very core of human nature in all its weakness, sinfulness, and growing pains as the only, unique, and full expression of God's own reality and self-communication. It follows then that all aspects of the world and of life contain within them the tangible flesh of the Word of God.

We all need to be convinced that the sacred and the secular are no longer "over against" each other, as though the divine were a superior counter-attraction to the "merely" human. This false notion springs from a graceless dualism. For many centuries we have been using a kind of language and a set of concepts in which the secular means "that which is not holy". What is now needed is a shift in our images and vocabulary so as to interpret the secular (in this case the independent autonomy and total humanness of each student in swiftly changing times) in terms of emergence and identity, and conceive of Christianity as the force and grace which will remind, enable and compel the secular to be truly itself – the holy work of God from the beginning.

There is nothing or nowhere, in fact (except, perhaps, in a state of deliberately chosen lovelessness) that these hidden graces do not exist. In Christian education, all subject matter is revealed as transformed in the light of revelation. Where formal school work is concerned, for instance, the teaching of *every* subject across the curriculum would present unique opportunities for this revelation.

Painting a Bird in Flight

Many wise religious educationalists emphasise that without recourse to an artistic dimension in the stimulation of the sacramental imagination, our achievements will be very limited. The task is not simple; nor is there only one way. Sharing the mystery has been described as the attempt "to paint a bird in flight". We need to stay persevering, and very humble.

John Westerhoff, Professor of Religion and Education at Duke University, believes that religion belongs to the sphere of the unsayable. It is better sung than recited, better danced than believed, better painted than talked about. That is why religious education is dependent on the arts and why children can have religious experience, and, more importantly, can help adults who have become independent, rational, and productive to rediscover the holy. Even in pre-Vatican Council days, philosophers Bernard Lonergan and Jacques Maritain emphasized, in their references to the process of education, the necessary role of a free exploration of art and of the emotions. Lonergan claims that "the life we are living is a product of artistic creation" and that it is on the artistic, symbolic level that we live our full range of humanity, discovering that we can become "emergent, ecstatic, standing out . . . originating freedom" (Lonergan, 1993: 217). The theologian of beauty Hans Urs von Balthasar sees music as the most ineffable art because it is the most immediate. That is why he sees its role on the cusp between humanity and divinity. "Music is a borderland of the human," he wrote, "and it is here that the divine begins." He sees music, particularly Mozart's, as liminal, between that which can and cannot be spoken, between God and humanity, between Creator and creation (McCosker, 2005: 91).

How can students be inspired to express their inmost, spiritual potential while schools are driven by merit lists, points and league tables? "Were they (students) not able to be moved by wonder at the beauty of the world we live in, or the power of artists, musicians and stories of writers, they would live in an inner spiritual and cultural desert." (National Curriculum Council Paper 36). Aware of how current pressures can reduce teaching and learning to a merely cerebral exercise, many DfES papers encourage a more creative and imaginative use of life-themes and cross-subject weaving in an effort to restore a more whole-school energy and motivation.

You Teach Who You Are

The key to effective RE or catechesis does not lie in the crafting of the perfect curriculum or syllabus. We do not necessarily have to rewrite immediately, in the light of a theology of nature and grace and its accompanying sacramental imagination, an updated syllabus to procure the results we sincerely hope for. It is the catechist's own heart that must first be recreated; the teacher's own vision that must first be transformed. If it is true that "the teacher does not write on inanimate material, but on the very spirits of human beings" (Palmer, 1998: 2), then the writing must be written across the teacher's own heart first. Once God's signature is identified and cherished there, everything that springs from that place will be blessed. 'Where to begin?' the thirteenth/fourteenth-century mystic Meister Eckhart was asked. "Begin with heart."

A popular catch-phrase of the past held that "faith is caught, rather than taught". This is still substantially true. It does not always mean that the faith has to be taught as well as to be caught. In the graced teaching is the catching and in the catching is the teaching. In the blessed knowing is the loving and in the loving is the knowing. Wisdom is knowledge laced with love. When this is happening it is a dialogue of life.

But when does this dialogue happen? When is the vision caught? When are those seeds which hopefully blossom during the later life of the student, sown? If the communication methods of the Teacher himself are anything to go by, it primarily happens in one of those potentially Emmaus moments, when "heart speaks to heart". "The old order has gone, and a new order has begun" (2 Cor. 5.17).

Know Yourself Well

Because we are all wonderfully designed by God, so carefully and lovingly put together, we have astonishing capacities to influence and transform each other at profound levels of our living. It is like a vibrant network of mutual interconnectedness, a flow of energy and inner power that began in creation and was revealed and personified in Jesus at the Incarnation. A theology of nature and grace concerns itself with such graced experiences in the unfolding of our humanity and of creation itself, an unfolding that is the continuing fleshing out in time and space of the implications of the once-for-all moment when God became human. When it comes to effective formation and teaching, so much depends on the authentic humanity of the educators.

In other words, the catechist can only be really present to someone else to the same extent as she is present to herself. She can only understand another to the same extent as she understands herself. She can only walk the Emmaus journey with others to the extent that she has walked it within her own heart. It is only when she has travelled the twists and turns of the labyrinth of her own holy mystery that she can be a grace for another in her teaching and in her presence. Good teaching, as we have touched on, cannot ever be reduced to the latest curriculum or set of sacramental guidelines, or pedagogical technique. It comes from the self-knowledge, the authenticity and integrity of the teacher and the catechist. Every major document on the effectiveness of Christian education in all its forms insists on that non-negotiable premise.

Know yourself, because you teach and catechize who you are. *Jesus revealed that true ministry is found only in the individual and community that can accept their own vulnerability. We all find that a hard thing to do; and so does the institutional church itself. But we have no choice about this principle. It is the way of Incarnation.* In a national address to Catholic teachers in 1996, Bishop David Konstant reminded them of

> the great need to integrate wholly what we believe with how we live. In Christian teachers there is need for real personal integration and harmony, so that the truth we teach is a genuine reflection of the person that we are.

He went on to quote Pope Paul VI (2002: 41): "Modern man listens more willingly to witnesses than to teachers, and if he does listen to teachers, it is because they are also witnesses."

Forging in the Smithy of the Soul

Thomas Groome (2003), senior professor of theology and religious education at Boston College, USA, explores the notion that "the heart of education is the heart of the educator". The transforming energy of teaching and learning is subtle and spiritual. Groome writes of St Augustine's understanding of the teacher within each person, proposing that when we learn something, the "real" teacher is not the teacher on the outside but the one inside. He refers to Parker J. Palmer, an internationally respected educational expert, who has taken the Augustinian proposal one step further by explaining that "the teacher within the teacher awakens the teacher within the student". Maybe this is another way of emphasizing the biblical belief in the notion of "heart speaking to heart"?

Carol Barry (2003), a lecturer in theology and religious education at St Patrick's College of Dublin University, quotes Palmer too:

> Spirituality – the human quest for connectedness – is not something that needs to be brought into or "added to" the curriculum. It is at the heart of every subject we teach, where it waits to be brought forth. . . . How can we take heart in teaching once more so that we can, as good teachers always do, give our heart to our students? How can we who teach, reclaim our hearts, for the sake of our students, ourselves, and educational reform?

In his celebrated *The Courage to Teach*, Palmer insists that teaching, like any truly human activity, emerges from our inwardness, for better or worse. The way we teach reflects the state of our own hearts and souls. Enabling and inspiring catechists and teachers is not always about providing maps, charts and syllabuses. It mostly consists in helping them understand that the essential teaching flows from the quality and integrity of their own inner life. "Teaching holds a mirror to the soul. Knowing myself is as crucial to good teaching as knowing my students and my subject. When I do not know myself, I cannot know who my students are." (Palmer, 1998: 2) But knowing and being who you are require relentless effort across the span of life.

Midwives of Mystery

There are many striking titles with which to honour catechists and teachers. They all reveal a range of roles that come into play when the adventure of education is undertaken. One of these roles is the privileged, difficult work of discovering and revealing the image of God in students of all ages. That is why teachers and catechists may be celebrated as *midwives of mystery;* they bring God's beauty to birth in those they serve.

Once a catechist sees her work along these lines of meaning, once her understanding of her ministry is perceived in these images of bringing something precious to birth, then everything about her presence to her students will be transformed. But first the veils must be parted for her own vision to be clear and focussed. Without that first transformation in her own heart, there will be no wonder for her students to catch. "First *become* the change you want to see in the world," said Gandhi; the rest follows.

In a somewhat similar way, the teacher and catechist can be called *prisms of love* as they reveal the colours of God in everybody and everything in the life of the student. As a prism reveals the colours of the spectrum in ordinary white light, the enlightened teacher will draw out from the hearts of the students, the rainbows of originality waiting to be released. For such a catechist even the most "ordinary" moments will become near-occasions of grace – "turn but a stone and start a wing". In this sense the teacher can also be called a *minder of thresholds*. Even where experiences may be seen as negative or even destructive, they can still be identified as places of grace. These can be hugely significant moments of breakthrough in the lives of young and old. God can only deal with reality. The mystics held that every moment is a gateway to heaven, a threshold to God's heart. This holds true for all the subjects taught, and all the experiences that happen, in the context of school and parish.

Co-creators with God is a beautiful title for all those workers in the vineyard. The catechist and teacher, by inspiring creativity and imagination in each student, empower them to be the prophetic voice of a Christian counter-culture, to be reflective and critical in a world that so easily loses its way and its wonder. *Agents of transformation* is another appropriate name for those committed to establish the reign of God. What is hoped and prayed for is a transformed attitude to life on the part of the students, a longing for true ecumenical and inter-faith trust and harmony in a suspicious religious milieu, a new vision about the holiness of the earth, a passion for identifying the conformity and consumerism all around us, and a yearning for peace in a world of wars.

The Spirituality of Teaching and Catechizing

Christian education in all its modes and models is always meant to be about the growth, development and journey of the whole human person towards abundant life, as a unique creation made in God's image. "At the heart of Catholic education and catechesis lies the Christian vision of the human person, of the entire potential of every student, made, as each one is, in the image and likeness of God" (Catholic Church. Bishops' Conference of England and Wales, 2000). Therefore, whenever a teacher is opening the mind and heart of a child or adult to the wonder of themselves and of nature, no matter what the topic, content or context, or whenever she is carefully and lovingly attentive to each one's needs, she is, in fact, and often unknowingly, uncovering for another the holiness of every moment; she is completing the work of Jesus in incarnating God more fully into this world.

To facilitate young people's growth in wisdom and age is to watch the unfolding of God in our midst. To see a child smiling as it manages to tie a lace or a ribbon for the first time, pronounces or spells a new word, sings a new note or learns to tell the time, is to see something of the joy of the incarnate God. When a pupil shyly says hello to a new classmate, the rejoicing Holy Spirit is again at work. All such moments of breakthrough into fresh connecting and understanding are essentially moments of wonder. The transcendence by the child of each of its formative stages of development is a sacrament of divine energy that is worthy of special notice and celebration.

When teachers believe that their ministry of teaching is about revealing the divine humanity within each student, then, already, the whole enterprise is seen to be sacred. To enter this sacred work wholeheartedly the teacher must be forever open to the self-transformation that gives inspiration and confidence to the emerging vision of the students.

Note

1 A fuller treatment of the many doctrinal, liturgical, and pedagogical issues that arise in the pursuit of this dynamic vision is available in O'Leary, 2008.

References

Barry, C. 2003. 'Spirituality and the Educator', in Prendergast, N., and Monahan, L. (eds). *Reimagining the Catholic School.* Dublin. Veritas.

Bruner, J. 1960. *The Process of Education.* Cambridge, MA. Harvard University Press.

Catholic Church. Bishops' Conference of England and Wales. 2000. *Religious Education in Catholic Schools: A Statement.* London. Catholic Media Office.

Catholic Church. Congregation for the Clergy. 1998. *General Directory for Catechesis.* Rev. ed. Dublin. Veritas.

Catholic Church. Sacred Congregation for Catholic Education. 1977. *The Catholic School.* Abbots Langley. Catholic Information Office.

Groome, Thomas. 2003. 'Forging in the Smithy of the Teacher's Soul', in Prendergast, N., and Monahan, L. (eds). *Reimagining the Catholic School.* Dublin. Veritas: 35–45.

Himes, M. 2006. 'Communicating the Faith: Conversations and Observations' in Imbelli, R. (ed.) *Handing on the Faith: The Church's Mission and Challenge.* New York: Crossroad.

Lonergan, B. 1993. Doran, R. and Crowe, F. eds, *Collected Works of Bernard Lonergan: Topics in Education* ed. R. Doran and F. Crowe. Toronto. University of Toronto Press.

McCosker, P. 2005. 'Blessed Tension: Barth and von Balthasar on the Music of Mozart', *The Way* (October).

National Curriculum Council. 1993. *Spiritual and Moral Development: A Discussion Paper.* National Currriculum Council.

O'Leary, D. 2008. *Begin with the Heart.* [Book and DVD.] Blackrock, Co. Dublin. Columba Press.

Palmer, Parker J. 1998. *The Courage to Teach: Exploring the Inner Landscape of a Teacher's Life.* San Francisco, CA. Jossey-Bass.

Paul VI (Pope). 2002. *Evangelii nuntiandi.* London. Catholic Truth Society.

CHAPTER ELEVEN

"LIKE A JAR OF WINE LEFT IN ITS PLACE FOR A WHILE . . . CLEAR, SETTLED AND PERFUMED"

EVAGRIUS OF PONTUS AND THE PURIFYING ENGAGEMENT OF STILLNESS

DAVID TOREVELL

In the Children's Society report *A Good Childhood* the authors identify some important strands of educational and social provision that need to be addressed if young people's well-being and flourishing are to be maintained and enhanced in the twenty-first century. After extensive research, they suggest that in a "competitive age" where "excessive individualism" frequently leads to the erosion of trust in others, a number of individual, educational, and social strategies need to be put in place. In countering such competitive pressures, their primary focus is on how human flourishing and happiness depend substantially on "fulfilling our capacity to live in harmony with others and with ourselves" (Layard and Dunn, 2009: 9). Young people require both outer and inner harmony, the report claims. What is particularly noteworthy in the findings is the importance placed on self-knowledge as it impinges on the emotional and spiritual lives of young people. Feelings clearly govern behaviour and psychological states, so it is essential that children learn to understand their own emotions and develop strategies for managing them – what the Report refers to as the promotion of their "better self". The report contributors go on: ""it is essential that children learn to understand their own emotions and develop strategies for managing their emotions and for cultivating the positive parts of their nature" (Layard and Dunn, 2009: 80).

The Report also shows how an essential constituent of harmonious living is the fostering of a balanced and positive appreciation of the world and the self which, in turn, leads to the living of a moral life. Anyone unsettled by the disturbance of negative emotions like anger or greed will find it difficult to aspire to important values even if in principle they subscribe to them

(Layard and Dunn, 2009: 79). One significant recommendation for fostering such understanding is the meditative practice of silence. Periods of silent sitting which help pupils reflect on their inner selves and how thoughts and feelings arise are strongly recommended; the authors refer to a school which has been successful in integrating this into their culture. Silence, they argue, is a well tested practice for promoting attention to the inner self and how one's emotional life is being conducted and there is ample evidence to suggest that such silent sitting improves well-being, inner calm, and the ability to deal with the vicissitudes of life (Layard and Dunn, 2009: 9). The formation of the attentive self through silence and stillness, therefore, is one challenging but democratic way of inculcating a watchfulness of the emotions which leads to happiness and fulfilment. This costs nothing in material terms. Scrutinizing and developing the inner life might cost in other ways, especially in confronting and examining one's own internal life battles, but these costs are generously repaid as you become "the captain of your soul" and are able to "treat the misfortunes of life as opportunities to rise to a challenge" (Layard and Dunn, 2009: 84), rather than as fruitless frustrations. The report endorses such self-knowledge as crucial if any real contribution to the needs of others is be forthcoming and effective. The moral advantages of stillness are made clear here.[1]

This chapter takes the recommendations of the report a stage further by focussing on what living in harmony with oneself might mean, why it is important and what strategies might help to foster its attainment. In particular, it centres on the therapeutic nature of the experience of stillness and silence by referring to the work of the fourth-century Christian monk Evagrius of Pontus, a choice which I hope to persuade you is not as unusual as it might first appear. I intend to show that the rich heritage of the monastic tradition, filtered through the lens of one remarkable monastic practitioner, has much to offer contemporary educational theory and practice. I take it as axiomatic that Evagrius' advice to his fellow monks about the attainment of *apatheia* (stillness) is as pertinent to twenty-first-century struggles as it was to his own monastic community of Nitria in northern Egypt in the fourth century.

Formation into Stillness

Formation into the ways of stillness is central to Evagrius' understanding of the monastic life. Note, says Evagrius, "how a jar of wine left in its place for a while to lie unmoved renders the wine clear, settled and perfumed"

(Sinkewicz, 2006: 8). Those things which upset this state of stillness (which prepares and allows for an experience of the Trinity and knowledge of what is real) are to be persistently resisted and avoided, since stillness does not come easily and needs to be prepared for like a good business man organizing his affairs. A determination to resist the attacks made on this space of potential freedom is essential. For example, the common problem of *acedia* – the feeling of sadness and listlessness coupled with the temptation to relax or abandon one's ascetic practices – is to be confronted with "the radiant beauty of perseverance" (Sinkewicz, 2006: 35). In a section on human relationships from his *Foundations of the Monastic Life*, Evagrius also exhorts his listeners to be aware of those who cannot achieve stillness, those who are "distracted" and move others away from "the science of stillness" (Sinkewicz, 2006: 8); "distracted" people are prone to drag others into their deceits; therefore, vigilance is required. The strategy of living in "voluntary exile" separate from the world is one method of protecting the stillness required for moral growth – location is important. He advises that

> The person who lives with those who are material-minded and involved in business affairs himself shares completely in their circumstances and becomes enslaved to human impositions, idle conversations, and all sorts of other dangers – anger, sadness, madness over material things, fear, and scandal. (Sinkewicz, 2006: 7).

Although this is not possible for many in the contemporary world, the need to withdraw, if only for a brief time, to a quiet place is an essential aspect of attaining the stillness Evagrius recommends.

The goal to be sought by a monk is *apatheia,* a resolute stillness freed from the unguarded and unbalanced attacks of the emotions and the passions, often regarded in early monasticism as external demonic attacks to be confronted and overcome (see Brakke, 2006). The demons produce in us passions like gluttony, fornication, avarice, anger, and resentment. These "thicken" the mind and stop people praying as they ought to and move them away from seeking the Word of God (Sinkewicz, 2006: 198). This is not an exercise in marginalizing or repressing the emotional life, but of bringing it into order and equilibrium so that the emotions might be realigned with and integrated into one's nature. It is an exercise in harmonious living as recommended by the Children's Society report. But we need to be careful about using too freely vocabulary about the emotions and reinserting it into 4th-century understanding, for Evagrius in his writings emphasized the occurrence of "thoughts" (*logismoi*) rather than emotions.

Let us explain a little more about this important distinction. The achievement and regulation of stillness for Evagrius is in direct proportion to a person's ability to deal with "thoughts". These arise disturbingly in the mind and heart, are associated with demons, and need to be dealt with in a disciplined and systematic way. The virtuous life is always intimately associated with this struggle and consists in having done battle with the "thoughts" : "The heart that does not have experience of warfare is deprived of the state of virtue, for 'virtue' (*aretē*), is the name of the action that comes from the word 'deeds of valour' (*aristeia*)" (Sinkewicz, 2006: 31). Virtue, therefore, *is* the name for engaging in those much needed battles with the "thoughts". Training in this way of valour is therefore crucial, for one "caught without training" is easily dragged down as one unprepared for an assault (Sinkewicz, 2006: 30). However, like a determined and strong athlete who has trained well, the monk is the one who "runs towards the beauteous and noble trophies of the practice of stillness. For how beauteous and noble is the ascesis that leads to stillness, how truly beauteous and noble!" (Sinkewicz, 2006: 5). It is only through "ascetic labours", therefore, that one is made resolute and these constitute the "honour" of the monk (Sinkewicz, 2006: 31).

"Thoughts" are associated with the old or false self which must be struggled against if a new self in Christ is to be formed. Our contact with the material world inevitably means we will be affected by it, sometimes in negative and destructive ways, and one clear symptom of this contact is the arousal of unsettling "thoughts". Such weakness should not be regarded as sin, but rather as the emergence of an unhelpful thought due in large part to our human vulnerability. However, once I begin to watch the "thoughts" arise, I can observe them and in time, with increasing stillness, they will disappear. The spiritual challenge is, as we have already seen, contextualized in terms of warfare and battle and it is not an easy struggle to win; a lack of stillness prolongs inner battles: "he who does not preserve stillness brings warfare to his soul . . . the person who loves stillness guards the senses and makes war on thoughts" (Sinkewicz, 2006: 40). Such language of making war on "thoughts" reflects Evagrius's firm conviction that one of the most debilitating states humans have to endure is the invasion of the heart by distracting "thoughts"; without the pursuit and achievement of stillness there is very little chance that human flourishing and moral growth will occur.

The "Thoughts" of the Fragile Self

The "thoughts" which arise come from without and cause unrest are better understood as symptoms of human fragility and vulnerability, almost involuntary eruptions brought about by living in the world. Evagrius did not believe that "thoughts" were sins, but simply symptoms of the fragility of human living in the world. Tilby reminds us that having such thoughts is not culpable in itself. They might become sin if surrendered to, but they are not the same thing. She comments, "Evagrius is clear that the thoughts are not themselves sins" (2009: 59). This is notably different from St Augustine's darker understanding of human nature which tends to conflate "thoughts" directly with sin, or at least temptation to sin, resulting in a view that having a wicked thought is the same as having a wicked heart. In other words, he encourages the identity of the thought with the sinful self, rather than acknowledging the *provisionality of such thoughts* and encouraging a freeing and detachment of oneself from their grip through the practice of stillness. Believing that the "thoughts" are external to the self, Evagrius taught a more positive view of human nature than St Augustine, even if he knew through his own experience of living the monastic life that the self was fragile and vulnerable and that outer temptations emanating from the material world could easily lead one away from the contemplation of God. As Tilby comments, "The point is that Evagrius expects *logismoi* to occur, but because he puts their origin outside the self he enables his followers to resist them without necessarily identifying with them or indulging them" (2009: 59–60). What was required was an attentive awareness and intimate knowledge of the thoughts or vulnerabilities and a humility to acknowledge how they affect the stillness of the heart. Evagrius exhorts his monks to note carefully the complexity of the "thoughts", their periodicity, the demons which cause them, the order of their succession and the nature of their associations. Then let him ask Christ for help with these "thoughts" (Tilby, 2009: 59).

Evagrius was influenced by the Stoics in his understanding of the distinction and relationship between "thoughts" and emotions since they distinguished between a full-blown passion, for which the rational person is responsible, and an involuntary preliminary motion (*propatheia*), which can lead to a unhelpful passion (Brakke, 2006: 54). Evagrius named "thoughts" "protopassions" which, if left unguarded, may change into negative emotions. At times "thoughts" can mutate into obsessive fantasies and here Evagrius rehearses some of the language of modern psychotic disorders which lead to self-destructive patterns of behaviour, although it is dangerous to read back modern into Evagrius' contemplative theology contemporary post-Darwinian psychological theories about sublimation and repression. Evagrius sees "thoughts", therefore, as "first movements" (Sorabji, 2000: 359); they are involuntary and it is common to find oneself being affected by them. However, it is up each person whether they persist and stir up negative emotions. Origen was the first theologian responsible for making the distinction in his biblical exegesis. Those scriptural passages which referred to Jesus' emotions like anger or distress, were considered to be "protopassions", since Jesus would never have had emotions in the Evagrian sense for he was without sin.

Consequently, "thoughts" might be best described as preliminary temptations which if succumbed to turn into sins of which one is culpable. It was Evagrius' disciple John Cassian (360–430) who made known to the Western Church through his *Institutes* and *Conferences* the eight "thoughts" which became transmuted into a system of numbered vices. DeYoung is right to suggest that Evagrius was "more interested in describing the guises of the demons and how to fight them than setting down a comprehensive list" (2009: 27). By the time of Pope Gregory the Great (540–604), "thoughts" started to be registered as "capital" or "principal" vices and had been paired down to seven by collapsing sloth into sadness, adding envy, and making pride the root of them all. It was St Thomas Aquinas who was to extend commentary on the vices with an important section on the issue in his *Summa theologiae* which became widely used after his death. But what was more significant about all these developments was the way in which "thoughts" became sins. Gregory the Great made this link explicit by writing that "'For a monk sin is assent to the forbidden pleasure of the thought" (Sorabji, 2000: 360); his formulation of "seven principal vices" which emerged from pride was to change the way Christians understood sin; during the medieval period the language of the seven principal sins, accompanied by a whole raft of ecclesial laws and punishments, strongly affected the manner in which clergy and laity viewed notions of temptation, offences against God, and individual salvation. By the thirteenth century the vices were well known to lay people as well as theologians and clerics, for their naming was to underpin much penitential practice. Although DeYoung reminds us that during the Middle Ages the vices "had become primarily a practical and pastoral tool not a theoretical construct" (2009: 30), the labelling of the seven as "capital vices" was to undergo another change not envisaged by Aquinas when they became referred to later by the Catholic Church as "deadly sins" to remind people of their seriousness and their association with mortal sin (which severed our relationship with God) rather than venial sin which was less drastic. This was a long way from the involuntary arising of "thought" as conceived by Evagrius and tells an interesting history.

The Blossoming of *Theoria Physike* (Contemplation) and Love

Another consequence of these historical developments was that notions of sin became inseparable from human identity. As Tilby points out, this transmutation of Evagrian "thoughts" into understanding of human nature as sinful was a considerable leap to take since it implied existential repercussions concerning what constituted human nature (2009: 24). After Augustine sin is no longer the result of outer demonic attack, but a part of what it means to be human and fallen: "Sin is not just what we do but what we are" (Tilby, 2009: 22). Christ is the only human being without sin. Later these moral failings became translated into a codified list of sins, but originally their appearance was a spur to ask questions of them and to subdue them. Instead of learning from them and asking Christ what they meant, the Christian Church changed them into sins of which we became ashamed. For Evagrius, the arising of such disquieting "thoughts" ought not to be identified with permanent constituents of the defining self, but as temporary aberrations, which if watched can be dealt with and seen as temporary and fleeting conditionings. This chapter suggests that the Evagrian conceptualization of the fragility of humanity is more helpful to pupils than later Christian formulations about sin and indeed many contemporary monastic writers tend to take his theology as their starting point.[2]

For Evagrius the emphasis given to the recognition and controlling of "thoughts" was significant since the moral and spiritual life could not be lived without such attention. The state of being which "is devoid of the passions and an unpossessive love for the whole of creation" is the beginning of a life formed by Christ, for obstacles are removed to allow the flourishing of the self (Tilby, 2009: 8). *Apatheia* involves both the cessation of wrongdoing *and* the attainment of inner serenity. And it blossoms naturally into agapç – unconditional love. But if this goal is to be reached, an "ascetic practitioner" must be practically engaged in the struggle to understand himself and the demonic attacks he is prone to. Alongside this constant warfare, Evagrius believed that it was possible to find peace of soul or heart by what he calls the "labours of asceticism" which included fasting, manual labour, lack of possessions, and prayer. The armoury of "true prayer" allows a person to turn away from mental representations tied to the passions and is "an impassible habit, which by means of a supreme love carries off to the intelligible height the spiritual mind beloved of wisdom" (Sinkewicz, 2006: 198). As I have already said, the aim of such disciplined practices was to gain "true knowledge of the things which exist" and of the Trinity. An epistemology of stillness is therefore set forth as being essential, for without its attainment no spiritual change can occur.

Clearly influenced by Origen, Evagrius showed how despite humanity's falling away from God it is possible to return to an original unity with the divine. Such teaching was partly based on Evagrius' own spiritual struggles. According to the Coptic version of Palladius' *Life of Evagrius*, he would regularly lead all-night discussions on Saturday evenings in which monks would reveal their troubling thoughts and discuss methods of dealing with them (Brakke, 2006: 50–51). Evagrius lists eight "thoughts" – gluttony, lust, avarice, sadness, anger, sloth, vainglory, and pride – arguing that "All the generic types of thoughts fall into eight categories in which every sort of thought is included" (Sinkewicz, 2006: 97). Evagrius shared with the Stoics the thought of sadness but not pleasure, desire, and fear. Three of the eight are more damaging than the rest – gluttony, love of money, and vainglory – and were formulated from Evagrius' own life experience and Bible stories, particularly the temptations of Jesus in the wilderness. This naming of the "thoughts" is part of the winning of the battle, since to identify them is to have control and mastery over them. "Thoughts" emanate from the perception of and involvement in the sensible world, clouding the mind and heart whose most natural state is contemplation, awareness, and delight in the divine.

According to Evagrius, human beings, like angels and demons, had originated as pure intellects in contemplation of God, a state from which they had fallen. Demons are full of anger and twisted with ignorance, their central aim being to attack the goodness of human beings which they observe with precision and envy. Human beings could easily slip into demonic ways of behaving since it is easy to become the very thing we rail and fight against and it took humility to accept this. Like the Platonists, Evagrius believed the soul is not fully rational. It has two irrational parts – a concupiscible or desiring part and an irascible or aggressive part. Since some of the "thoughts" originate from these parts and because of the soul's distinctive make-up, a monk cannot simply eliminate the energies they produce (Brakke, 2006: 53). Instead they must be redirected "'according to nature" into positive virtues: "The goal of practical knowledge is to heal these irrational parts of the soul, so that they produce not negative emotions but the positive virtues" (Brakke, 2006: 53). The intellect is the rational part of the person, but this also is susceptible to vainglory and pride; however, once purified it produce its own virtues – prudence, understanding, and wisdom, argues Brakke (2006: 53). The attainment of *apatheia*, therefore, entailed freedom not from psychic energy itself (which is a constituent of our human nature) but from the misdirection of such energies into negative emotions via "thoughts". Not unlike the suggestions made in the Children's Society report, strategies must be put in place to direct our psychic energies into positive rather than harmful ways of thinking and doing. Energy itself is neutral. For Evagrius, too, demons are not from another supernatural world, but embedded in the stuff of creation and the cosmos; the battle going on in the monk's heart was part of a much wider cosmic battle taking place in everyday life – in communities and households and creation generally. External to the self, strategies were needed for dealing with and outmanoeuvring their subversive wiles. Evagrius believed the monk's task was to bring creation back to God by holding it in unity in his own heart. But first the heart needs to be cleansed of those things which disturb its natural state of calm. This is the contemplative goal – to erase the disturbances of the heart so that it might be at one with divine creation. As Tilby observes, the meaning of spiritual practice was to clear the "heart from evil – *praktike* – then to engage in natural contemplation – *theoria physike*" (57).

The heart is the central arena in which the race for the trophy of stillness is run. It is both location and judge, for the heart that learns stillness learns to discern the thoughts which arise. "Judge the thoughts in the tribunal of the heart" commands Evagrius (Sinkewicz, 2006: 38). This overcoming of the "thoughts" does not entail repression of the emotional life, but a gradual becoming aware and distancing from them. Ignatius of Antioch used the word *apatheia* to refer to his calm acceptance of Christ's suffering, and for Clement of Alexandria this stillness echoed the calmness and freedom of God himself. To be still is to have the freedom and joy God possesses. It is characterized by a selfless love which allows the person to be unconditioned by anxieties and worries which tie down and imprison the self. A well planned war, therefore, was indispensible and had to be fought with a sophisticated knowledge of one's enemy, otherwise stillness would not be maintained. Knowing the enemy was a step towards defeating him. As Brakke comments:

> For the Evagrian monk knowledge was power. By gaining increasingly precise knowledge of the demons – their identities, their characteristic

> strategies, their interrelationships, their origin and nature – the monk gained mastery over them and over his responses to them. (2006: 52).

But peace of mind and heart, as I have indicated earlier, did not come easily and involved a rigorous training of the heart which encouraged a stable and contemplative approach to the world once the passions had been overcome.

Stillness and Contemporary Education

What then, has a fourth-century monk to do with modern educational theory and practice and in particular the well-being and flourishing of young people? I hope my detailed analysis has persuaded you that Evagrius offers insight, advice, and diagnosis about the emotional life which is not only relevant to his own monastic community in fourth century but to pupils and teachers today. His advice may be tailored judiciously to a range of diverse school and college contexts. Of course, some of his anthropological understandings are no longer sustainable, especially his belief in the external, cosmic force of demonic attacks, but these can easily be laid aside to discover the continuing benefits and relevance of Evagrius' teaching for contemporary pedagogical practice.

Perhaps the first and most important is his emphasis on an epistemology of stillness. Evagrius reminds us that it is impossible to know the world unless the disquieting "thoughts" and emotions which been accrued through contact with the material world, start to be settled and we can begin to "'see" again the world from a mind and heart free of the "passions". Standing free of material concerns so that we may become strangers to conditioning processes allows us to cultivate stillness and thereby a more contemplative approach to the divine, the world, and the self. A parallel method has been advocated before, of course, particularly through the important work of Hammond et al. (1990: 6–7) who wish to connect ordinary human experience to religious experience by the involvement of pupils in key spiritual "exercises"; their methodology of exploring the spiritual dimension of pupils' lives by taking a experiential approach extends the phenomenological by including ways of appreciating the *intentions* of religious people. Their aim, as they write at the start of the book, is to offer a set of "exercises which . . . will be useful to teachers who want to help their pupils or students to understanding something of ways in which people with spiritual or religious belief experience the world" (Hammond et al.,

1990: 6). They do not, however, advocate that teachers generate "religious experience" in the classroom.

Their section on raising awareness is one which concerns this chapter most directly and in their concentration on the practice of "stilling" reiterate what Evagrius and many religious traditions have highlighted for centuries:

> Most of the time we are not really aware of the bustle of sighs, sounds, and sensations that are crowding into our awareness both from outside and inside our bodies. From the religious person's point of view, this low level of awareness is a kind of blindness, which gets in the way of important exercises like prayer, meditation or the attentive performance of ritual . . . In certain kinds of Buddhism, awareness meditation is the central religious practice, whilst in Western religion, the Bible teaches believers to "be still and know that I am God". (Hammond et al., 1990: 57)

Grimmitt astutely writes that by taking this approach "There was . . . a clear assumption that ordinary and sui generis religious experience are part of the same continuum" (Grimmitt, 2000: 33). Exercises are recommended to help pupils situate ordinary experience against wider religious horizons, a point the authors make explicit when they suggest that by exploring silence pupils learn to be aware of "the here-and-now of their experience, to discover awe and wonder in themselves . . . and to reflect on these realities in the light of metaphors and expectations of the (religious) believer" (Hammond et al., 1990: 23). Nevertheless, by simply offering exercises to assist pupils in making connections between ordinary and religious experience is no guarantee of their effectiveness and some of the difficulties with this approach centre on making the crucial transition from reflecting on personal experience to exploring its equivalent in religious experience – or indeed, perhaps more importantly, helping pupils realize that the practices themselves are potentially religious, a notion the authors never really expand upon. And in any case, any such transitions are not likely to be as smooth as the authors envisage. If explicitly religious material does not accompany the methodology throughout and offer a clear religious contextualization, then what is likely to occur is an exploration of the inner self without any religious understanding of the experience; one might then wonder why any such exercises take place in RE classes at all![3] Again, as Grimmitt points out,

> It is noteworthy that in the project's main teaching resource, out of 231 pages only 12 refer to the use of explicitly religious material. While the

> weakness is not insurmountable, it does confirm the project's tendency to give too little importance to the place of learning about explicit religious traditions in RE. (Grimitt, 2000: 34). What I am suggesting here counters some of the criticisms of Hammond et al.'s approach, since I advocate that pupils' experience of stillness and silence should always be made in explicit relationship to those major religious traditions – and that of practitioners like Evagrius – whose spiritual practices have been developed over time and culture. What I want pupils to know and feel is that stillness and silence practices *per se* have often been regarded as important religious activities and by their involvement in such, they will inevitably join a long tradition of spiritual formation (see Davies and Turner, 2008; Foster, 2009; Lash, 2006; Steindl-Rast, 1999).

Second, silence and stillness cut us off, for at least a little while, from the noise of the world and teach us that we can live in freedom if we make the effort. But the onus starts and ends with us. This "noise" may come in the form of a bombardment of images and sounds simply as we make our way through any day, but these need and should not determine the manner in which we live and perceive our lives. Third, the emphasis Evagrius gives to the watching of our own hearts, besides being a useful exercise in concentration, begins to purify the heart and to help pupils gain a sense of intimacy with the divine. God is discovered through and in the heart's purification. Becoming aware of those "thoughts" which arise within us, and preventing them from becoming disturbing "emotions" which control our reactions to others, allows pupils to approach life in a more balanced and appreciative manner. Any formation in stillness is the beginning not only of wisdom and love therefore, but of finding in the world a place we can call home. Fourth, through perseverance and practice, pupils learn what the meditative body has to teach and grow in an appreciation of the relationship between bodily posture, discipline and happiness. It is not unusual for pupils to admire athletes who live on a strict diet and follow a disciplined training programme. Why should religious training be any more alarming to pupils?

Fifth, pupils begin to see that their own "thoughts" of anger or lust or sloth are not constitutive elements of their definitive character, but temporary aberrations which can be fought, overcome, or at least redirected into positive feelings. There is no fatalism of identity here. The challenge is to know and name such "thoughts" and not to fall victim to them. To achieve this is to have power over them. Sixth, the explanation of the relationship between "thoughts" and emotions given by Evagrius undermines the somewhat darker Augustinian language of sin and fall which has assumed a too lofty position in the Christian tradition. The language of temptation and sin might not be appropriate for all pupils and Evagrius gives us freedom to balance such language with his emphasis on the vulnerability rather than self-loathing of our fallen human nature. Consequently, this ancient yet contemporary approach to well-being encourages pupils in their return to their most natural state of being – the contemplative – with the important corollary that pupils become aware that the divine is not situated at the end of philosophical speculation or ecclesial doctrine, but known and felt within the gradually purifying heart. The goal is one which pupils will come to realize is worth all their efforts, for, as Evagrius tells us, it brings its own rewards : "Sweet is this life, the practice of it a delight" (Sinkewicz, 2006: 5).

Notes

1 It is not only during childhood and adolescence that practices of watchful silence are recommended. On 5 January 2010 the Mental Health Foundation launched a campaign to make mindfulness courses based on silent meditation available on the NHS. Due to the increase of depression among adults and the limited effects of antidepressants, such strategies are being recommended as the way forward (see 'Meditation on prescription: charity urges alternative remedy for depressed patients', *The Guardian* 5 January 2010: 4). For an account of the relationship between mental health and meditation within religious practices (especially Buddhism) see Davidson and Harrington, 2002.

2 One example would be Thomas Keating, the contemporary American Trappist monk, who follows in the monastic tradition of Evagrius. He writes that the

> spiritual journey does not require going anywhere because God is already with us and in us. It is a question of allowing our ordinary thoughts to recede into the background and to float along the river of consciousness without noticing them, while we direct our attention to toward the river and watching the boats go by. If we stay on the bank, with our attention on the river rather than on the boats, the capacity to disregard thoughts as they go by will develop, and a deeper kind of attention will emerge. (Keating, 2006: 35).

Later in the same text he writes about the practice of contemplation in relation to thoughts which appear in our consciousness:

> Any perception that arises from any one of the senses or from the imagination, memory, or reason is a thought. Hence, whatever the perception may be, let it go. Everything which registers on the stream of consciousness will eventually go by, including the thought of self. It is just a question of allowing every thought to go. Keep your attention on the river rather than on what passes along the surface. (Keating, 2006: 41)

See also Merton, 2007: 221–224.

3 It is worth noting that the fast growing Mindfulness in Schools project attempts

to introduce into classroom pedagogy the practice of mindfulness, often based around the exercises of meditation and silence, but without any explicitly religious framework. Although it clearly draws from the contemplative religious traditions of the past, it communicates its aims and practices in the largely secular terms of well-being and mental health and as an effective means to combat stress, depression, and eating disorders. It will be interesting to see whether schools which adopt this approach in the future choose to align it directly to religious education.

References

Brakke, D. 2006. *Demons and the Making of the Monk.* Cambridge, MA. Harvard University Press.

Davidson, R. and Harrington, A. (eds). 2002. *Visions of Compassion: Western Scientists and Tibetan Buddhists Examine Human Nature.* Oxford. Oxford University Press.

Davies, O., and Turner, D. 2008. *Silence and the Word: Negative Theology and Incarnation.* Cambridge. Cambridge University Press.

DeYoung, R.K. 2009. *Glittering Vices: A New Look at the Seven Deadly Sins and Their Remedies,* Grand Rapids, MI. Brazos Press.

Evagrius. 2003. *Evagrius of Pontus: The Greek Ascetic Corpus,* trans. R. Sinkewicz. Oxford. Oxford University Press.

Foster, D. 2009. *Deep Calls to Deep: Going Further in Prayer.* London. Continuum.

Grimmitt, M. 2000. *Pedagogies of Religious Education: Case Studies in the Research and Development of Good Pedagogical Practice in RE,* Great Wakering. McCrimmons.

Hammond, J.H. et al. 1990. *New Methods in RE Teaching: An Experiential Approach.* Harlow. Oliver & Boyd.

Keating, T. 2006. *Open Mind, Open Heart: The Contemplative Dimension of the Gospel.* New York. Continuum.

Layard, R., and Dunn, J. 2009. *A Good Childhood: Searching for Values in a Competitive Age.* London. Penguin.

Lash, N. 2006. *Holiness, Speech and Silence: Questions on the Question of God.* Aldershot. Ashgate.

Merton, T. 2007. *New Seeds of Contemplation.* New York. New Directions.

Sorabji, R. 2000. *Emotion and Peace of Mind: From Stoic Agitation to Christian Temptation.* Oxford. Oxford University Press.

Steindl-Rast, D. 1999. *A Listening Heart: The Spirituality of Sacred Consciousness.* New York. Crossroad.

Tilby, A. 2009. *The Seven Deadly Sins: Their Origin in the Spiritual Teaching of Evagrius the Hermit.* London. SPCK.

CONTRIBUTORS

Patricia Hannam has been working with philosophical inquiry in the classroom for many years. She is an experienced teacher, advisor, and trainer in religious education in P4C. Her doctoral research is into the role of inquiry in religious education in plural democracies. Her book *Philosophy with Teenagers: Nurturing a Moral Imagination for the 21st Century* was co-authored with Eugenio Echeverria of the Central American Centre for Philosophy for Children and Adolescents, and published by Continuum in 2009.

James D. Holt has been a teacher of RE for the past 12 years. He has worked as a Head of Department and Head of Faculty in two large Manchester schools. He was recently appointed as Senior Lecturer/Subject Leader in Religious Education at the University of Chester. He is currently studying for a PhD in interfaith relations at the same institution. He previously completed an MEd at the University of Birmingham where his thesis focussed on New Religious Movements in the secondary RE classroom.

Emma McVittie is a a senior lecturer in primary RE at the University of Cumbria and is also a free-lance primary RE consultant leading the local authority RE netwrok groups throughout Cumbria.She was previously a primary teacher. Her research interests include the use of reflection as a tool for learning within higher education and the use of problem based learning to explore issues in RE.

Heather Marshall has taught RE at a comprehensive school in South Liverpool fo rhte past five years, teaching pupils from diverse backgrounds across Key Stages 3, 4 and 5. Outside school she is an executive member of NATRE and represents them locally in Merseyside. She is the teacher representative on the Liverpool SACRE and works very closely with the local authority advisor to develop good RE across the city. She believes that RE learning should extend beyond the classroom and she therefore works closely with different community organizations such as Liverpool Community Spirit and various faith groups. In addition she has a number of academic RE interests, including recently becoming a Farmington Fellow which has enabled her to explore pedagogy and classroom practice more deeply. She is currently completing an MA in RE at Warwick University.

Daniel O'Leary is a priest, author, and teacher in the diocese of Leeds. As a curate and parish priest he has worked in parishes for 30 years. He taught theology and religious education at St Mary's University College, London and became chair of its Religious Studies department before being appointed Episcopal Vicar for Christian Formation in Leeds. An award-winning author of 12 books, he is a regular contributor to *The Tablet.* His most recent publication is *Begin with the Heart: Recovering a Sacramental Vision* (Dublin: St Columba Press, 2008).

Gaynor Pollard is a senior lecturer in Theology at Newman University College in Birmingham. She teaches across a range of disciplines, but has always combined academic study with religious education, including working as an RE advisor with the Diocese of Chester and as a PGCE programme leader at University College Plymouth, St Mark and St John. Her main research interest is religious education and violence, and she has recently co-edited two texts: *Hovering over the Face of the Deep: Philosophy and Theology with Children*, with Gertrud Yve Iversen and Gordon Mitchell, and *Religious Education and Christian Theologies: Some European Perspectives*, with Peter Schreiner and Sturla Sagberg.

Joy Schmack is director of RE Services at Liverpool Hope University. After teaching in schools in South London for 20 years she joined the Croydon Inspection and Advisory Service where she particularly focussed upon religious education, faith relations, and inclusion. As a chief examiner for GCSE Joy has written many textbooks and teacher handbooks. Her particular research interests include challenging misconceptions through religious education and raising standards at Key Stage 4.

Julian Stern is Dean of the Faculty of Education & Theology at York St John University, and is also Professor of Education and Religion. After teaching in schools in the South of England for 14 years, he worked in a number of universities prior to coming to York St John: the Institute of Education, London, the Open University, Brunel University, and the University of Hull. He has written many books and articles for trainee teachers, experienced teachers, and teacher trainers. Recent books include *The Spirit of the School* (2009), *Schools and Religions: Imagining the Real* (2007), *Teaching Religious Education: Researchers in the Classroom* (2006), and *Involving Parents* (2003).

Matthew Thompson is a part-time Senior Lecture in Religious Education at Liverpool Hope University. He is also Director of Liverpool Community Spirit, a unique community education partnership which for the past eight years has been promoting inclusive, caring community spirit in the heart of Liverpool through innovative adult learning programmes and an inter-faith youth council. He has published a number of papers, most recently in Michael H. Grimmitt (ed.), *Religious Education and Social and Community Cohesion: Challenges and Opportunities* (Great Wakering: McCrimmons, forthcoming 2010).

Rob Thorne has been Course Leader for Religious Studies at Oldham VI Form College for over ten years. During this period the department had grown extensively and achieved excellent results. Rob has been a mentor on the Manchester Metropolitian University Religious Studies PGCE programme, where he lectured on "Best Practice in A-Level Religious Studies". Rob has also been active in the College's wide-ranging engagement with the local community which contributed to Oldham VI Form College achieving Beacon status.

Dr David Torevell is Associate Professor in the department of Theology, Philosophy and Religious Studies at Liverpool Hope University. He has published two books on Christian worship, *Losing the Sacred: Ritual, Modernity and Liturgical Reform* (T&T Clark, 2000) and *Liturgy and the Beauty of the Unknown: Another Place* (Ashgate, 2007). He is presently completing a book on contemplative theology in relation to a re-reading of Samuel Beckett's *Waiting for Godot.* He has published numerous articles on his research interests which include liturgy, Christian spirituality and ethics, theological aesthetics, and Christian education.

Index